NUTSHELLS

The Irish Legal System

Round Hall's Nutshell, Nutcase and Exam Focus Series

NUTSHELL TITLES

Specially written for students of Irish law, each title in the Nutshell series from Round Hall is an accessible review of key principles, concepts and cases. Nutshells are both the ideal introductory text, and the perfect revision aid.

- **NEW – Criminal Law (2nd edition) by Cecilia Ní Choileáin**
- Tort – 2nd edition by Ursula Connolly
- Company Law – 2nd edition by Catherine McConville
- Constitutional Law – 2nd edition by Fergus Ryan
- Land Law by Ruth Cannon
- Contract Law by Fergus Ryan
- Equity Law by Karl Dowling
- Family Law by Louise Crowley
- Employment Law by Dorothy Donovan
- Evidence by Ross Gorman

NUTCASE TITLES

Round Hall Nutcases are written to give you the key facts and principles of **important cases** in core legal subject areas. Straightforward, no-nonsense language makes Nutcases an easy way to understand and learn key cases.

- Tort – 2nd edition by Val Corbett
- Criminal Law by Majella Walsh
- Evidence by Neil Van Dokkum

EXAM FOCUS TITLES

The series is especially designed to support students in the weeks coming up to exams by providing a unique tutorial approach to answering questions.

- Criminal Law by Sarah Carew

NUTSHELLS

The Irish Legal System

by

DOROTHY DONOVAN
LLB, LLM, Barrister-at-Law

ROUND HALL

THOMSON REUTERS

Published in 2010 by
Thomson Reuters (Professional) Ireland Limited
(Registered in Ireland, Company No. 80867. Registered Office
and address for service 43 Fitzwilliam Place, Dublin 2)
trading as Round Hall.

Typeset by Carrigboy Typesetting Services

Printed by ColourBooks, Dublin

ISBN 978–1–85800–594–2

A catalogue record for this book is available from the British Library.

I dedicate this book

to my beloved brothers,
the late John Donovan and the late Kevin Donovan.

They were twins, identical physically yet both very different and both,
unknowingly, had much to teach.

Contents

Table of Cases

IRELAND

England

United States

European Court of Justice

European Court of Human Rights

International Court of Justice

Table of Legislation

Constitution of Saorstát Éireann

The Irish Constitution

Irish Statutes

Irish Statutory Instruments

English Statutes

European Treaties

European Convention on Human Rights

International Treaties

Introduction to the Irish Legal System

Introduction

There are two main types of legal systems: a common law legal system and a civil law legal system (not to be confused with civil law which is a branch of law within the Irish legal system). Ireland has a common law legal system with a constitution and legislation. A civil law legal system is based solely on legislation. An example of a civil law legal system is the *Napoleonic Code*, or *Code Napoléon* (originally called the *Code Civil des Français*), established under Napoléon I in 1804.

Most, if not all, legal systems may be broken down into a series of rules that together form the legal system. These rules bestow rights and impose duties and obligations. In the Irish legal system, the origin of these rules may be traced back to either precedent, the Constitution or legislation. These three sources are the primary sources of law in our legal system and if a rule does not have one of these origins as its source, it is not law, albeit that it may resemble law. Consider, for example, the constitution, rules and regulations of clubs and associations.

There are also sources of law known as secondary sources. These secondary sources are custom and practice, academic writings and intellectual influences.

Sources of Law

A legal system is made up of a series of individual rules. Sources of law are the origins of these rules.

These individual rules form part of what we call *the* law. All of these rules have their own independent existence and can be traced to some primary source of law, be it our Constitution, legislation (national and EU) or precedent (case-law/judicial decision). It is through these sources that Irish law may be identified.

PRIMARY SOURCES OF LAW

As already noted, there are three primary sources of law in the Irish legal system.

1. The Constitution;
2. Legislation (national and EU); and
3. Common Law/Precedent.

EXAMPLES

- *Rule*: The personal liberty of citizens shall not be interfered with other than in due of course of law. This rule has its origin in Bunreacht na hÉireann 1937 (see Art.40.4.1° of the Constitution).
- *Rule*: It is against the law to drive when drunk. This rule has its origin or source in legislation—(see s.49 of the Road Traffic Act 1963 (as amended)).
- *Rule*: Member States of the EU are prohibited from engaging in anti-competitive acts. This rule has its origin or source in EEC/EU law (see arts 81 and 82 of the Treaty of Rome).
- *Rule*: It is against the law to injure your neighbour through negligence; the whole of the world may be your neighbour. (This is known as the *neighbour principle*.) This rule has its origin or source in precedent/the common law (see *Donoghue v Stevenson* [1932] A.C. 562).

The following is a brief description of each of the three primary sources of law:

1. The Constitution

The Irish Constitution is known as Bunreacht na hÉireann. In addition to the preamble, it contains a series of Articles, numbered from 1 to 63. It is the fundamental law of the State and prior to Ireland becoming a Member of the then European Economic Community in 1973, the Constitution was the supreme law of the land. (On the Constitution, see further at Ch.2).

2. Legislation

Legislation is law enacted by a legislature. In the Irish legal system, legislation is enacted by the Oireachtas or by the competent body of the European Union.

National Legislation

Legislation in Ireland may be primary legislation or delegated (secondary) legislation. Students should not confuse primary and secondary *legislation* with primary and secondary *sources* of law. Primary and secondary legislation are *both* primary sources of law. National legislation consists of Acts of the Oireachtas (sometimes referred to as statutes) or statutory instruments (which may be regulations or ministerial orders). Statutes are primary legislation whereas statutory instruments are delegated or secondary legislation. (On legislation, see further at Ch.3).

EU Law

Legislation of the European Union consists of the Treaties, Regulations, Directives and Decisions. Where there is conflict between this source of law and one of the other sources, EU law is supreme.

3. The common law

The term "common law" means the ancient unwritten law of England. It was called "common" because it was the law common to the whole of England and Wales. With the passage of time, common law came to mean judge-made law, which is also referred to as precedent. (Students should not confuse precedent in this sense with the doctrine of precedent per se—on the doctrine of precedent, see Ch.8). The common law was introduced in Ireland in 1210 by the then King of England, who decreed that the law known as the *common law* was to be applied throughout the Pale (the Pale was Dublin and those parts of Meath, Louth and Kildare within a 20-mile radius of Dublin). By 1331 the common law was extended to apply throughout the whole of Ireland.

SECONDARY SOURCES OF LAW

In the Irish legal system secondary sources of law are:

- Custom and practice; and
- Academic writings.

Custom and practice

Custom is a practice that has been followed in a particular locality in such circumstances that it is to be accepted as part of the law of the locality. If it was not law, why would it be consistently followed or practised? To be recognised as customary law it must be reasonable in nature and it must have been followed continuously as though of right since the beginning of legal memory. Legal memory dates back to 1189 but proof that a practice has been followed within living memory raises a presumption that it has been followed since time immemorial (1189).

Academic writings

The writings of such legal scholars as Lord Coke, Hale and Blackstone might in the absence of a primary rule be relied upon by a court, and are treated as authoritative to the extent that they may be equated to decisions of judges in cases before them in court.

Academic writings as a secondary source include law textbooks and law journals. For example, McMahon and Binchy's book entitled *Law of Tort,* 3rd edn (Dublin: Bloomsbury Professional, 2000) is continually referred to in court.

In addition to the secondary sources listed above international law and canon law may provide a secondary source of law. (On international law, see Ch.5 and on canon law, see p.11).

Secondary sources are not as important as primary sources and are only resorted to when there are no primary source materials available on a particular issue. They will be persuasive rather than binding on a court. See, for example, *RC v IS* [2003] I.R. 451 where the Supreme Court approved a passage from Shatter, *Family Law*, 4th edn (Dublin: Bloomsbury Professional, 1997)) when deciding what guardianship meant. This was subsequently applied in *FN and EB v CO* [2005] I.R. 311 and may then be relied on under the doctrine of precedent. (On Precedent, see further at Ch.8 see p.94).

THE IRISH LEGAL SYSTEM AND ITS DEVELOPMENT

The development of the Irish legal system may be traced through a pre-Norman period and a Norman period up to the current legal system. In the pre-Norman period the law in force was known as the *brehon law*. During in the Norman period, the common law was introduced.

THE BREHON LAW

In ancient Ireland, the *law* was extremely important. The law applicable initially in the country was known as the "Brehon Law".

The brehon law was a fully developed legal system based primarily on custom, and it existed long before the Christianisation of the country, associated with St Patrick in 432, and long before the invasion by the Danes or the Anglo-Normans. The brehon legal system was a system that required restitution for wrong rather than punishment. It was administered by itinerant justices known as brehons. The law was so revered and honoured that neither courts nor police were needed to enforce it. The brehon law remained in force throughout Ireland until it was abolished in the seventeenth century.

The brehon legal system consisted of two categories called Cain and Urradas. Cain was the law that applied to the whole of Ireland while Urradas applied to a locality and was the local law. Each locality and/or clan might have its own local law. In the event of conflict between *Cain* and *Urradas*, the latter took precedent. Since the Monasteries functioned as independent "clans", their laws were modified to suit the individual Bishop-in-charge and with the passage of time, canon law began to infiltrate the brehon legal system.

Brehon law covered civil, military and criminal law. It regulated social action from the ruler down to the slave and established their rights and privileges. In civil law there were detailed rules for such things as property management and industry. There were laws governing the relationships of landlord and tenant, the duties of father and son, and duties of foster-parents and foster-children. There were laws for distress or seizure of goods, laws for trespass, and laws for the giving of evidence. In the area of criminal law, offences and their penalties were minutely detailed together with the quantum of compensation which applied in respect of offences.

THE COMMON LAW

The common law is based on rules developed by the royal courts during the first three centuries after the Norman Conquest at the Battle of Hastings in 1066. It was called "common" law because it was applicable to the whole country as opposed to local customs. *Circa* 1172 the common law was introduced into Ireland by King Henry II.

The Normans' concern was mainly with the setting up of a central administration capable of safeguarding the royal revenues, and it was through machinery developed for this purpose that the common law developed. Royal representatives were appointed and detailed to tour throughout the shires (towns or boroughs) to see how the affairs in these shires were being conducted. This inevitably involved these local representatives participating in the work of the local courts. During the reign of Henry II (1154–1189), to whom the development of the common law is principally attributed, the royal representatives were sent out on regular tours. These tours were known as *circuits*. The functions of these royal representatives gradually became exclusively judicial and they became known as wandering justices or itinerant judges.

At this time the body of advisers to the King was known as *Curia Regis* (the Royal Court). Under the *Curia Regis* justices heard cases in London but also travelled through the kingdom twice a year. These travels were referred to as the *Assizes*. During the reign of Henry II two further courts were established; the Court of Exchequer and the Court of Common Pleas. The Court of Exchequer, which was set up to hear disputes concerning revenues, was the first permanent royal court and the Court of Common Pleas the second. The origins of the common law are effectively to be found in these two courts. With the success of these two courts a third royal court called the Court of King's Bench emerged.

The judges of the Court of Common Pleas superimposed a single unified system upon the multiplicity of local customs that had existed up until then. This was so successful that the judges of the Court of Exchequer joined in.

With the passage of time, common law came to mean judge-made law because decisions of judges in cases formed precedents for future cases. Common law doctrines, rules and principles of law were developed through these cases.

The commencement of common law proceedings in the courts was by means of a writ. Writs were commands in the name of the ruling Monarch. Writs were issued out of the Chancery by the Chancellor. In 1258 the ruling monarch, Henry III, was forbidden by the *Provisions of Oxford* to issue any new writs and writs then became a closed category.

The development of the common law and its courts in Ireland closely followed the English system. The common law in Ireland was significantly affected by the enactment of the 1937 Constitution. Article 15.2.1° of that Constitution provided that the "sole and exclusive power of making laws" for the State was vested in the Oireachtas. Thus, only the Oireachtas could now make laws for the Irish State. It follows from this that as far as the Irish legal system was concerned, the common law was frozen from that point in time because the common law, being law made by judges, would contravene Art.15.2.1°. Further, Art.50 of the new Constitution provided that laws that were in force prior to the enactment of the Constitution would be carried over only in so far as they were consistent with the Constitution.

With the passage of time, the common law became somewhat unsatisfactory for the following reasons:

(1) If a wrong was perpetrated and there was no writ covering that wrong, no action could be taken in the common law courts.

(2) The common law judges applied the rules and principles of law rigidly even where it did not do justice in a particular case and indeed led to an injustice.

(3) The sole remedy of the common law was damages (monetary compensation) and this remedy was not always appropriate.

EXAMPLE (1)

A, following negotiations with *B*, has entered into a contract with *B* to supply goods. The contract is duly signed/executed and afterwards it is discovered that there is an error in the contract. *A* still wishes to proceed with the contract as negotiated but *B* refuses by saying that *A* must either proceed with the contract as signed or otherwise he will sue *A* for breach of contract. What *A* wants is the remedy of rectification of the contract. There is no common law remedy allowing for rectification of a contract, and thus *A* is not only left without a remedy but may be sued for breach of contract and has to pay damages to *B*. Similarly *B* may wish to have the contract performed as signed and what he thus requires from the court is the remedy of specific performance. The common law has no such remedy and what *B* will get, if successful, is the remedy of damages.

EXAMPLE (2)

The plaintiff lives in a house near a quarry. This quarry has normally operated from 8am to 6pm but for the past year has carried on quarrying until well after midnight with the result that the plaintiff cannot sleep, and is constantly stressed from the serious noise pollution. This plaintiff in a common law court, if successful, would be awarded damages but the quarrying and the noise would continue. Thus, this remedy is not effective or appropriate in circumstances where what the plaintiff requires is for the noise to cease. What is needed is injunctive relief which the common law cannot supply.

It was as a result of these inadequacies that the courts of equity or chancery developed.

EQUITY

Equity is sometimes referred to as a gloss on the common law. It supplements the common law and was developed to remedy the defects of the common law. Equity represents an attempt to correct the rigidity that confronts all legal systems and results in the denial of justice by allowing wrongs to go without remedies.

Equity has a broad and narrow meaning. In its broad sense equity corresponds in a general way to natural justice. In the narrow sense equity is defined as those rules administered by the Court of Chancery.

Actions in the common law courts were commenced by means of a writ. If there was no writ covering the situation sought to be litigated, you were at common law left without a cause of action and thus without a remedy. Parties who found themselves in this position started petitioning the Chancellor. As an ecclesiastic, the Chancellor tended to decide these petitions on the basis of justice rather than in accordance with rigid and technical legal rules. The Chancellor started to issue remedies that were firstly in accordance with justice, and secondly and importantly more appropriate to the circumstances of the case. These remedies included injunctions, decrees of specific performance, rectification and rescission.

The Chancellor's court, which was independent from the common law courts, became known as the Court of Chancery and because of its flexibility became more popular than the common law courts. The Chancellor's court developed its own set of doctrines, rules, principles and *maxims*. The Chancellor acquired a permanent jurisdiction distinct from the common law courts.

The Courts of Chancery or courts of equity were for a time more satisfactory than the common law courts for the following reasons:

(1) If no common law legal rule was breached, a plaintiff could not take a case in the common law courts but that plaintiff could now seek relief in the Court of Chancery.

(2) Where the remedy of damages was inadequate or inappropriate, the Court of Chancery could supply, for example, the remedies of injunction, specific performance, rectification and rescission.

Thus, in our *Example (1)* above in equity *A* may be able to secure the remedy of rectification of the contract so that it provides terms as negotiated between parties or B may be able to secure a decree of specific performance.

In our *Example (2)* above equity could offer a remedy of injunction prohibiting the quarry from carrying out work after a certain hour in the evening.

THE FUSION OF THE COMMON LAW AND EQUITY

In England the common law and equity remained separate systems until the Judicature Acts 1873–1875 which fused the courts of the common law and equity. In Ireland the two systems were unified or fused by the Supreme Court of Judicature (Ireland) Act 1877. This unification gave greater benefit to litigants and was more satisfactory in that they could avail of both common law and equitable remedies in the one court. Thus in our example (2) above the plaintiff could not only obtain the remedy of damages but could in addition obtain injunctive relief. In other words, the plaintiff could avail of a combination of *both* remedies.

CLASSIFICATION OF LAW

INTRODUCTION

Law may be classified in many different ways.

Law may be *substantive* or *procedural* (adjectival). Substantive law is that part of the law that deals with rights, duties and all other matters that are not matters purely of practice and procedure. Procedural or adjective law is that part of the law that deals with practice and procedure in the courts, it is the machinery for getting matters into court and sets out how matters are to progress or be dealt with once in court.

Law may be *public* or *private*. As to whether a law is public law or private law is not always clearly defined and there may be times when they might overlap. Public law is, in the main, law concerned with matters pertaining to the State and matters with a significant interest to the public at large. Public law includes constitutional law, administrative law and criminal law. Private law, on the other hand, is concerned with the relationships between individuals in circumstances where there is no significant interest to the public at large. Private law includes contract law, property law, company law, and the law of torts. Within these categories of private law there are some further sub-divisions or categories such as employment/labour law, family law, commercial law, competition law and succession law.

Law may also be classified as *civil* law or *criminal* law. The law of tort, contract law, property law, company law and commercial law are examples of civil law.

Law may be further classified as *natural* law and *positive* (or positivist) law. Natural law has multiple meanings and is superior and antecedent to positivist law (law enacted by man). There are also various theories of natural law but two more generally accepted theories are the divine version and the version that arises by virtue of our human state or nature. The ancient Greek philosophers such as Socrates, Plato and Aristotle considered that there was a kind of perfect justice given to man by nature and that man's laws should conform as closely as possible to this. The divine or Christian version espoused by St Thomas Aquinas was that the ultimate authority was God, and natural law was a higher law and superior to positivist law, and that positivist law must not conflict with it, and that if it did conflict then it was not law properly so called. All natural law theories appear to have in common the concept that in order for laws enacted by man to be valid, they must conform with the basic principles of natural law and natural rights. In other words, a law that does not comply with natural law is invalid and thus does not require to be obeyed. Natural law seeks to introduce a moral element into law, however, some theorists say this moral element has no place in law. See, for example, the Lord Devlin and HLA Hart debate. Positivist law is law which is enacted by man. In Ireland the Constitution and legislation are examples of positivist law although the Constitution contains reference to natural law rights. See, for example, the preamble which states that all authority comes from the Most Holy Trinity and acknowledges that all obligations are to the Divine Lord, Jesus Christ. See also Art.40.1 which provides that, "[a]ll citizens shall, as *human persons*, be held equal before the law".

PUBLIC LAW

Public law includes the following:

Constitutional law

Constitutional law, as the name suggests, is law which flows from the Constitution. (See further, Ch.2).

Administrative law

Administrative law is the law that governs the administration of the State and the operation of the various governmental departments and public authorities such as local authorities.

Criminal law

Criminal law deals with conduct which is prohibited, in other words, conduct which is deemed criminal. Criminal law is concerned with law enforcement by the prosecution of offences and the imposition of penalties.

PRIVATE LAW

Private law includes the following:

Contract law

Contract law is the law that regulates or governs the consensual relationship between parties. Contract law through its body of common law decisions and statute law sets out rules under which it can be determined if a contract or agreement is binding, which contract or agreement ought to be enforced, what is to happen if a contract is breached, and what is to happen if a contract is silent on a particular matter.

Company law

Company law is the law that governs companies registered under the Companies Acts 1963–1990. Company law through its body of common law decisions and particularly through legislation sets out the formalities dictating how a company is incorporated and managed, inter alia, the number of directors the company must have, the number of members (share-holders), the holding of annual general meetings, ordinary meetings, the filing of annual reports and annual accounts, the liquidation or winding-up of a company, receivership and examinership. Company law also deals with corporate enforcement.

Property law

Property law is the law that deals with such matters as easements and profit à prendre. Examples of easements are rights of way, rights of light and rights of support. Examples of profit à prendre are the right to graze cattle, the right to take timber off land or the right to fish in a lake.

Law of tort

A tort is a wrongful act or omission for which damages (compensation) may be obtained in a civil action in court by the person who suffered the wrong against the person who caused the harm (the tortfeasor). Negligence, professional negligence, nuisance, trespass and defamation are examples of torts. A private wrong may also constitute a public wrong; for example, false imprisonment may also be a criminal offence.

Canon law

Canon law is that body of law made by or adopted by ecclesiastical authority, for the governance of its church and its members. The word "canon" is derived from the Greek *kanon*; a rule or practical direction that acquired an exclusively ecclesiastical signification. Canon law is also called "ecclesiastical law", however, strictly speaking, there is a slight difference of meaning between the two expressions in that ecclesiastical law refers to all laws made by the ecclesiastical authorities whereas canon law does not.

The Rule of Law

The rule of law is fundamental to a democratic order. It is sometimes referred to as the principle of legality. Central to the rule of law is the notion of limited governmental power. Rights or entitlements of persons and obligations imposed on persons must be set out in legal form and may only be altered in the manner set down in law.

The essential characteristics of the rule of law are:

- Nobody is above the law, including individuals and government. Thus, the law is supreme.
- The law is based on a concept of justice which emphasises interpersonal adjudication, standards and the importance of procedures.
- There must be an underlying moral basis for law.
- Laws must be published and available.
- Laws should not be vague.
- There must be an independent judiciary.
- Judicial precedent.
- Common law methodology
- Legislation should be prospective and not retrospective. Law which applies to past events is to be avoided.

The Constitution

2

Introduction

The Irish Constitution is called Bunreacht na hÉireann. Bunreacht na hÉireann means Basic Law of Ireland. The Constitution is the basic or fundamental law of State. It is a primary source of law in the Irish legal system and is subject only to our obligations under European Union law.

Bunreacht na hÉireann was enacted in 1937 in a plebiscite held on July 1, 1937 and came into operation on December 29, 1937. It replaced the Constitution of Saorstát Éireann 1922 (the Constitution of the Free State of Ireland).

The 1937 Constitution states clearly that the source of authority in Ireland is the people of Ireland. The preamble to the Constitution states clearly: "We the people of Éire ... Do hereby adopt, enact, and give to ourselves this Constitution". It is only the people who, by referendum, can amend any of the provisions of the Constitution or add new provisions to it.

The Constitution has an Irish version and an English version and if there is any conflict between these two versions the Irish version takes precedence.

The System of the Constitution

As already noted, the Constitution is laid out in a series of 63 Articles and a preamble.

The preamble

A preamble is not an essential element of a constitution, thus, some constitutions do not have one. The preamble reflects the historical, religious, social, political and economic context in which the Constitution was enacted. The preamble has been held by the courts to be more than aspirational in nature. See *Russell v Fanning* [1988] I.R. 505 and *McGimpsey v Ireland* [1990] 1 I.R. 110; [1990] I.L.R.M. 440.

The articles of the Constitution

The following is a brief description of the content of the Articles of the Constitution:

The nation and the State

Articles 1–11 deal with the national right to self-determination, the national territory, the name of the State, the nature and character of the State, the institutions of the State, the powers of Government, the national flag, the language of the State, nationality and citizenship, natural resources, and the revenue of the State.

The President

Articles 12–14 deal with the office of President, the functions of the President, the removal of the President, the Presidential Commission, and the appointment and resignation of a President.

The national parliament

Articles 15–19 deal with the constitution of and the procedures and privileges of the National Parliament. Article 15 bestows the sole and exclusive legislative power on the National Parliament.

Legislation

Articles 20–27 deal with legislation and with the legislative process, the promulgation of laws, constitutional text, referral of Bills to the Supreme Court and referral of Bills to the people.

The Government

Articles 28–29 deal with the Government itself, the appointment of a Taoiseach (Prime Minister) and a Tánaiste (Deputy Prime Minister), war and national emergency, responsibility of Government to Dáil Éireann, international relations and international agreements and importantly, Art.29 deals with Ireland's membership of the European Union.

Other constitutional organs

Articles 30–33 deal with the office of the Attorney General, the Council of State and the Comptroller and Auditor General.

The courts

Articles 34–39 deal with the establishment of the courts, the jurisdiction of the courts, the judiciary (appointment and removal of judges and the independence of the judicial function), judicial review of legislation, the trial of offences and fair procedures in criminal trials.

Fundamental rights

Articles 40–44 deal with fundamental, human or personal rights. These rights may be numerated or unenumerated.

Directive principles of social policy

Article 45 deals with the State's undertaking to promote, as far as practicable, the welfare of the people by securing and protecting a social order in which justice and charity shall inform all the institutions of the national life.

Amendment of the Constitution

Articles 46–63 deal with how the Constitution may be changed by referendum, continuance of laws and constitutional transition.

Fundamental Rights in the Constitution

Introduction

Articles 40–44 guarantee certain rights referred to as human or fundamental rights; these are rights that people are entitled to by virtue of being human and include such rights as:

- equality before the law;
- the right to life and person;
- the right to one's good name;
- the right to life of the unborn;
- the right to personal liberty;
- property rights;
- the right to inviolability of the dwelling;
- freedom of expression;
- freedom of assembly and freedom of association;
- family rights;
- rights regarding education; and
- rights regarding religious freedom.

The source of these rights is said to be natural law which is superior and antecedent to man-made law and that the Constitution merely acknowledges and confirms these rights rather than being the grantor of them.

These human or fundamental rights are not absolute; they can be limited or restricted by the Oireachtas on the grounds, for example, of the common good or public order. See, for example, *Ryan v Attorney General* [1965] I.R. 294.

They may also be delimited by people's own actions. See, for example, the decision of the High Court, upheld by the Supreme Court, in *Murray v Ireland* [1985] I.R. 532; [1991] I.L.R.M. 465 where the High Court said that although citizens had the right implied under the Constitution to procreate, the plaintiffs in this case had delimited this right by their own criminal actions. The plaintiffs who were husband and wife were in separate prisons serving life sentences.

It has been held that not all constitutional rights are equal and that there is a hierarchy of rights. If there is a conflict between constitutional rights, the courts will look at all the circumstances and weigh all of the factors to decide which constitutional right takes precedence. See *People (Director of Public Prosecutions) v Shaw* [1982] I.R. 1 where a person's right to life was held to rank higher in priority than the accused's right to fair pre-trial procedures.

Not every fundamental right is expressly set out in the Constitution. There are many rights such as the right to bodily integrity, the right to marital privacy, and the right to earn a livelihood that are not specifically stated in the Constitution. These are rights which have been implied into the Constitution by the courts.

Constitutional rights may be numerated (also referred to as express or specified) and unenumerated (also referred to as implied or unspecified).

NUMERATED RIGHTS

Numerated rights are those rights that are expressly set out in the Constitution. They are:

- Equality before the law—Art.40.1: See, for example, *O'G v Attorney General* [1985] I.L.R.M. 61 where the court held that s.5 of the Adoption Act 1952 which prevented childless widowers from adopting while imposing no similar condition on childless widows breached the equality guarantee in Art.40.1.
- The right to life and person—Art.40.3.2°: The right to life has never been specifically invoked although it was mentioned in some cases. See, for example, *G v An Bord Uchtála* [1980] I.R. 32. The right of personal protection is also guaranteed under this Article. See *State (Burke) v Lennon* [1940] I.R. 136.
- The right to one's good name—Art.40.3.2°: See *State (Vozza) v Floinn* [1957] I.R. 227.
- The right to life of the unborn—Art.40.3.3°: See *The Attorney General (Society for the Protection of Unborn Children (Ireland) Ltd) v Open Door Counselling Ltd* [1988] I.R. 593; and *Attorney General v X* [1992] 1 I.R. 1.

- The right to personal liberty—Art.40.4.1°: This right provides that your right to personal liberty may only be interferred with in due course of law. Laws that limit personal freedom are such laws as the Mental Health Acts and criminal law which allows for imprisonment. See, for example, *State (Burke) v Lennon* [1940] I.R. 136.

- Property rights—Art.40.3.1°–2° and Art.43: These Articles protect property (real and personal). There has been much debate as to whether these Articles are simply a duplication of each other. One view is that one Article protects the right to own property whereas the other Article protects rights over that property which is actually owned. One of the first cases on property rights to come before the courts was *Buckley v Attorney General* [1950] I.R. 67—the *Sinn Féin Funds* case. See also, *Attorney General v Southern Industrial Trust* (1960) 94 I.L.T.R. 161; and *Central Dublin Development Association v Attorney General* (1975) 109 I.L.T.R. 69.

- The right to inviolability of the dwelling—Art.40.5: This right guarantees that no person is to come into your home without your consent, unless authorised by law. Generally the consent must be express. However, in the case of *DPP v Forbes* [1994] 2 I.R. 542 it was held that householders give an implied consent to the Gardaí to enter the curtilage of their homes to ensure enforcement of the law. This implied consent may be withdrawn by the householder. See *DPP v Molloy,* unreported, High Court, January 26, 2000. On the right to inviolability of the dwelling see *Director of Public Prosecutions v McMahon* [1986] I.R. 393.

- Freedom of expression—Art.40.6.1°.i: See *Attorney General v Paperlink Ltd* [1984] I.L.R.M. 373.

- Freedom of assembly—Art.40.6.1°.ii: This right may be limited in the interest of peace and order. See *People (Director of Public Prosecutions) v Kehoe* [1983] I.R. 136.

- Freedom of association—Art.40.6.1°.iii: This right is the right, for example, to join a trade union. It can also be considered the right to disassociate; in other words the right not to join a trade union should you so wish. See *PMPS v Attorney General* [1983] I.R. 339.

- Family rights—Art.41: These rights, which are limited to the family based on a marriage recognised by Irish law, protect the institution of marriage and bestow certain rights and obligations on parents. These rights are stated to be inalienable (cannot be given away) and imprescriptible (cannot be taken away or lost by failure to exercise except in very limited circumstances under the Adoption Act 1988 and where an order of the High Court is necessary).

- Educational rights—Art.42: The right under this Article guarantees that the State will provide for a certain minimum level of education. Minimum has been held to mean primary education. This Article also specifies that parents are the primary educators of their children and thus may educate them at home or in schools other than state schools provided that children receive a certain minimum level of education. Cases of relevance are *Crowley v Ireland* [1980] I.R. 102; *Jamie Sinnott v Minister for Education* [2001] 2 I.R. 505; and *O'Sheil v Minister for Education* [1999] 2 I.R. 321.
- Freedom of religion—Art.44: This Article provides that the State guarantees to respect and honour religion. It gives express recognition to some religions. Much of the earlier case law on this right concerned the religious education of children of mixed marriages. See, for example, *In Re Tilson, Infants* [1951] I.R. 1.

Unenumerated rights

Unenumerated rights are those rights which have been implied into the Constitution by the courts. These rights which are not a closed or exhaustive category and which have been implied into Art.40.3.1° and Art.40.3.2° include:

- The right to bodily integrity—*Ryan v Attorney General* [1965] I.R. 294. This case is considered to be the seminal case on unenumerated rights. The court in this case recognised that there was such a right as the right to bodily integrity and that the fluoridation of water by the State was a breach of this right. However, because the fluoridation was held to be in the interest of the common good, the fluoridation was nonetheless constitutionally permissible.
- The right to marital privacy—*McGee v Attorney General* [1974] I.R. 284. In this case, the court said there was implied into the Constitution a right to marital privacy and that this right included the right of marital parents to decide the size of their family. *Norris v Attorney General* [1984] I.R. 36 sought unsuccessfully to extend this right to decriminalize homosexual acts between consenting adults.
- The right to work and to earn a livelihood—*Murtagh Properties v Cleary* [1972] I.R. 330. In *Murphy v Stewart* [1973] I.R. 97 the Supreme Court accepted the proposition submitted on behalf of the plaintiff that among the unspecified personal rights guaranteed by the Constitution is the right to work. See also *Cafolla v O'Malley* [1985] I.R. 486. The right to a livelihood is not an unqualified right to a particular livelihood—see *Attorney General v Paperlink Ltd* [1984] I.L.R.M. 373.

- The right to litigate and have access to the courts—*Macaulay v Minister for Posts and Telegraphs* [1966] I.R. 345, where the court said that the right to have recourse to the court to defend and vindicate a legal right is one of the personal rights of the citizen included in the general guarantee of Art.40.3. See also, *Byrne v Ireland* [1972] I.R. 241; and *O'Brien v Keogh* [1972] I.R. 144. Again like all rights, the right to litigate and have access to the courts is not an unlimited right—see, for example, *DK v AK* [1993] I.L.R.M. 170 where the court said the citizen's right of access to the courts must be read subject to the judicial power to strike out an action where there is an abuse of process.

- The right to fair procedures—*In Re Haughey* [1971] I.R. 217. This right has frequently been regarded as part of the latent content of Art.40.3 and applies in both civil and criminal proceedings.

- The right to travel within the State has been held to be a corollary of the right to personal liberty guaranteed by Art.40.4; see the dictum in *Ryan v Attorney General* [1965] I.R. 294 where Kenny J. gave the right of free movement within the State as an example of one of the many personal rights of the citizen which flow from the Christian and democratic nature of the State.

- The right to travel outside the State and the ancillary right to a passport—see *State (M) v Attorney General* [1979] I.R. 73 where Finlay J. in the High Court stated that these rights are one of the hallmarks which are commonly accepted as dividing states which are categorised as authoritarian from those which are categorised as free and democratic. Therefore, there is no doubt that these rights are the personal rights of each citizen, subject to the guarantees provided by Art.40, although not enumerated there.

- The personal rights of the unmarried mother in regard to her child. The rights that the marital parents hold under Art.41 are also rights of the unmarried mother and her child. However, they are rights implied under Art.40.3 rather than under Art.41 which limits the rights to the family based on marriage. See *G v An Bord Uchtála* [1980] I.R. 32; and *State (Nicolaou) v An Bord Uchtála* [1966] I.R. 567.

- The right to communicate—*State (Murray) v Governor of Limerick Prison*, unreported, High Court, August 23, 1987. See also, *Attorney General v Paperlink Ltd* [1984] I.L.R.M. 343 where the court said the very general and basic human right to communicate must be one of those personal unspecified rights of the citizen protected by Art.40.3.1°.

Review of the Constitution

The Constitution has been the subject of periodic review. What emerges from the reviews, including the more recent ones by the Constitution Review Group and the two All-Party Oireachtas Committees, is that the Constitution is a fundamentally sound document that commands the respect of the people and serves them well. However, the reviews suggest that in addition to the amendments already carried out, some further amendments are necessary or desirable in order to renew the Constitution fully.

In 1966, an informal Oireachtas committee undertook a general review of the Constitution and issued a report a year later.

In 1968, a legal committee chaired by the Attorney General, produced a draft report.

The 1972 Inter-Party Committee on the Implications of Irish Unity addressed constitutional issues in relation to Northern Ireland. Its work was continued by the 1973 All-Party Oireachtas Committee on Irish Relations and later by the 1982 Constitution Review Body (a group of legal experts under the chairmanship of the Attorney General). None of these three groups published a report.

The New Ireland Forum was established in 1983. Its report in 1984 covered some constitutional issues.

In 1988 the Progressive Democrats published a review entitled *Constitution for a New Republic.*

In 1994 constitutional issues with regard to Northern Ireland were again addressed by the Forum for Peace and Reconciliation established by the Government. The Forum suspended its work in February 1996 but met once more in December 1997.

In 1995 the Constitution Review Group was established by the Government. Its remit was to review the Constitution, and in the light of the review, to identify those areas where constitutional change may be desirable or necessary, with a view to assisting the All-Party Oireachtas Committee on the Constitution. The Constitution Review Group published its report in July 1996. The All-Party Oireachtas Committee on the Constitution 1996–1997 published two progress reports in 1997, the All-Party Oireachtas Committee on the Constitution 1997–2002 published five progress reports and two commissioned works, and the All-Party Oireachtas Committee on the Constitution 2002 has to date published two progress reports.

The reviews and political experience have identified seven major sources for constitutional change. These are:

1. Northern Ireland;
2. The European Union;
3. International human rights developments;

4. Socio-economic change;
5. Working experience of the Constitution;
6. Outmoding of some provisions of the Constitution; and
7. Inaccuracies in the text of the Constitution.

Very much to the fore is also the need for a provision giving express rights of the child rather than the present situation whereby the rights of the child are seen as ancillary to or as a corollary of parental rights.

CONSTITUTIONAL INTERPRETATION

If there is doubt or ambiguity as to the meaning of a word or phrase in a provision of the Constitution, it falls to the courts to interpret that word or phrase or indeed the provision itself.

The extensive case law on interpretation of the Constitution indicates that there are five different approaches to constitutional interpretation used by the courts. These approaches are:

(1) The literal approach;
(2) The broad approach;
(3) The harmonious approach;
(4) The historical approach; and
(5) The natural law approach.

Of the five approaches, the literal approach and the broad approach are currently the main approaches used by the courts. However, it must be stated that the courts sometimes use a combination of the various approaches.

The literal approach

According to this approach, which is a textual approach, because the Constitution is the fundamental law of the State, it must be construed according to the words which are used and these words, where their meaning is plain and unambiguous, must be given their literal meaning. However, the Constitution must also be construed as a whole and thus, where there is doubt or ambiguity, regard may be had to other provisions and the state of the law when the Constitution was enacted. See *State (Browne v Feran)* [1976] I.R. 147; and *DPP v O'Shea* [1982] I.R. 384.

In *DPP v O'Shea* [1982] I.R. 384, a case dealing with a right of appeal from the High Court to the Supreme Court, the court said that the phrase in Art.24.4.3° of the Constitution providing that an appeal "from all decisions of the High Court" prima facie should be given its literal meaning and that there were no other meanings for the purpose of the case before the court.

The broad approach

This approach, while it favours a process of interpretation which is guided by the actual language of the text of the Constitution, rejects the excessive reliance on a literal interpretation preferring instead a purposive approach. This approach looks to the purpose of the provision in issue. See *Attorney General v Paperlink Ltd* [1981] I.L.R.M. 348 where the court held that the Constitution "is a political instrument as well as a legal document and in its interpretation the courts should not place the same significance on differences of language used" in different paragraphs of an Act but should use a "purposive rather than a strictly literal approach to the interpretation".

In *Dillane v Ireland* [1980] I.L.R.M. 167, the meaning of the words "the State in its enactments" in Art.40.1 were examined and whether the District Court Rules were state enactments for the purpose of Art.40.1. Giving a broad interpretation, the court said that District Court Rules were state enactments because they came into existence as a result of a Ministerial order or a statutory instrument, enacted pursuant to statute.

The harmonious approach

Basically the harmonious approach may require a modified understanding of part of the text of the Constitution. This approach is also referred to as the "Doctrine of Harmonious Interpretation". Under this doctrine, constitutional provisions should not be analyzed in isolation from all the other parts of the Constitution but should be construed so as to harmonise with the other parts. It presumes that the drafters of the Constitution had one scale of values and wished those values to permeate evenly and without internal discordance throughout the Constitution. See again, *Dillane v Ireland* [1980] I.L.R.M. 167 where the court said that the doctrine of harmonious interpretation required, where possible, that constitutional provisions be construed and applied so that each would be given due weight in the circumstances of the case.

In *Twomey v Ireland* [1985] I.R. 532 the Supreme Court agreed that where a literal interpretation would produce absurdity and conflict with other provisions, a harmonious approach should be used whereby the Constitution must be read as a whole and its various provisions not looked at in isolation.

A judicial view has emerged that some Articles of the Constitution are more important than others, that there is a hierarchy of rights and in the case of conflict one right will take priority over another. See *State (Ryan) v Lennon* [1935] I.R. 170; and *People (DPP) v Shaw* [1982] I.R. 1.

The historical approach

This approach requires judges to consider the state of affairs, legal as well as extra-legal (political and social for example) at the time the Constitution was enacted. See *In Re Article 26 and the Offences Against the State (Amendment) Bill 1940* [1940] I.R. 470 where the court said that before dealing with the relevant Articles a judge must essentially consider the state of the law at the time of the drafting and enactment of the Constitution. If legislation which must have been within the knowledge of the framers of the Constitution and yet they did not put an express provision in the Constitution prohibiting such legislation then considerable weight must be given to this fact. In other words, the drafters of the Constitution were aware of the existence of this type of legislation and if they were not in agreement with it or thought it contrary to the Constitution, they would have inserted an express prohibition against such legislation. In *Melling v Mathghamhna* [1962] I.R. 1; and *Conroy v Attorney General* [1965] I.R. 411, where it was held that the state of the law at the time of the enactment of the Constitution was a factor to be taken into account when deciding whether a crime was minor or not, the Constitution itself had not defined what was a "minor" crime.

This approach obviously does not take into account social and moral changes in society with the passage of time but then, it is the *historical* approach.

The natural law approach

This approach works on the basis that there are certain rights that are so fundamental that they are immutable or cannot be changed by constitutional amendment. See *State (Ryan) v Lennon* [1935] I.R. 170 where the court said that certain rights were so fundamental as to be beyond the power of the Oireachtas to abridge by way of amendment of the written Constitution.

This approach acknowledges that there are natural rights or human rights not created by law and that the Constitution merely acknowledges or confirms their existence and gives them protection, and that these rights exist independently of the Constitution. See *Murphy v PMPA Insurance Co* [1978] I.L.R.M. 25 where the court held that it is well established that certain natural and personal rights may exist side by side with the Constitution although not specifically referred to or comprehended in the Articles of the Constitution.

In *Ryan v Attorney General* [1965] I.R. 294 the High Court said that there are many personal rights of the citizen which flow from the Christian and democratic nature of the State and which are not mentioned in Art.40 of the Constitution at all, such as the right to free movement within the State and the right to marry.

In *State (Ryan) v Lennon* [1935] 69 I.L.T.R. 125, a provision allowing an amendment of the Constitution by way of legislation was condemned. The court used a natural law interpretative approach.

Legislation

Introduction

Legislation is the laying down of legal rules by a competent authority which in Ireland is the Oireachtas. In Ireland legislation is a primary source of law. Subject only to European Union law and the Constitution, legislation is our most important source of law.

The power to make laws for the State is vested solely in the Oireachtas (Art.15.2.1° of the Constitution). Legislation that conflicts with the Constitution is invalid (Art.15.4.1°).

Legislation may be primary legislation or secondary legislation. Statutes or Acts of the Oireachtas are primary legislation and statutory Instruments are secondary legislation. Statutory instruments are Ministerial regulations, Ministerial orders, rules or bye-laws. Secondary legislation is also referred to as delegated legislation. (Note: Both primary legislation and secondary legislation are a *primary* source of law).

There are other quasi-legal instruments known as schemes, administrative rules, Ministerial circulars and codes of practice. If these are made pursuant to a power under statute, they will have legal status unless the statute in question expressly provides otherwise.

As already noted, legislation is made or enacted by the Oireachtas whereas statutory instruments are made pursuant to a power delegated by the Oireachtas usually to a government minister. The power is delegated in a statute, referred to as the Parent Act.

The Legislative Product

The legislative product in Ireland consists of Acts or statutes and statutory instruments.

Statutes

Statutes are, as previously mentioned, primary legislation. Statutes include Acts of Parliament (the Oireachtas), Acts of the Parliament of Saorstát Éireann (1922), and Acts from 1226 to 1922 which have not been repealed.

When a statute and its amending statutes are gathered together into one Act, it is called a consolidated Act. See for example, the Taxes Consolidation Act 1997.

Citation of statutes

This simply means what an Act or statute is called (its title) and how it may be cited. An Act will have a long and short title.

> **EXAMPLE**
>
> Companies Act 1963:
> An Act to Consolidate with Amendments Certain Enactments Relating to Companies and for Purposes Connected with that Matter [*23rd December, 1963*] is the long title for this Act but s.1(1) of that Act states "This Act may be cited as the Companies Act, 1963".

Layout of statutes

Layout or division of statutes means how the statute is arranged, set out or its format.

Statutes are divided into what are referred to as sections, subsections, paragraphs and sub-paragraphs. Each section is given a number and each subsection within that section is numbered. Long statutes, in addition to being arranged in sections, subsections, paragraphs and sub-paragraphs, may also be arranged in what is referred to as "Parts". Parts are numbered.

There may also be schedules attached to an Act. Schedules deal with ancillary matters or list earlier statutes repealed or amended by the present statute.

STATUTORY INSTRUMENTS

Statutory instruments, as already noted, are secondary or delegated legislation.

The Statutory Instruments Act 1947 defines a statutory instrument as every "order, regulation, rule, scheme or bye-law" made in the exercise of a statutory power. Statutory Instruments are law laid down by a body or a person, usually a Minister of Government, to whom the superior legislature, the Oireachtas, has delegated the power to make such law. The power will be delegated by the "Parent Act".

Delegated legislation is sometimes used to flesh out the detail of the Parent Act. For example see the Organisation of Working Time Act 1997 which is an Act regulating the amount of hours to be worked, the amount of holidays due, holiday pay, and rest breaks. It would be too cumbersome to put all the detail into the main Act. Further this type of detail may change on an on-going basis. Thus, for example, a statutory instrument entitled Organisation of Working Time (Determination of Pay for Holidays) Regulations 1997 (S.I. No. 475 of 1997) sets out how pay for holidays is to be determined.

However, when power is being delegated via a statutory instrument there is a constitutional limit on that power. In *Cityview Press Ltd v AnCO* [1980] I.R. 381 the Supreme Court said that the test as to whether delegated power is constitutional or not is whether the power is no more than merely giving effect to principles and policies which are contained in the Parent act. This test is referred to as the "principles and policies test".

Citation of statutory instruments

Statutory instruments are cited by their name, followed by their S.I. number.

> **Example**
>
> Local Government (Planning and Development) Regulations 1990 (S.I. No. 89 of 1990).

Layout of statutory instruments

Statutory instruments are generally arranged in the same manner as statutes with an explanatory memorandum at the end.

Some statutory instruments may be short, being merely a few pages while others are very long. See for example, the Rules of the Superior Courts 1986 (S.I. No. 15 of 1986) which is a major tome consisting of in excess of 170 pages.

The Legislative Process

So, how is legislation made? The legislative process is governed by Arts 20–27 of the Constitution.

A statute starts life as a draft statute and is referred to as a Bill. A Bill must go through a procedure in the Houses of the Oireachtas (the Dáil and the Seanad) before becoming an Act. Once the Bill has been passed by both Houses and is signed into law by the President it is known as an Act. Once a statute is enacted it remains in force until it is repealed.

There are different types of Bills:

- Ordinary Bills;
- Bills to amend the Constitution;
- Taxation Bills;
- Abridged-Time Bills; and
- Private Member's Bills.

Bills may also be Public Bills or Private Bills. In the main, Bills are Public Bills.

PUBLIC BILLS

Public Bills, with the exception of Consolidation Bills, go through five stages in the House in which they are initiated. Acts, other than a Money Bill, may be initiated in either House.

First stage

At the first stage the Bill is essentially proposed and voted on. When a Bill is initiated in the Dáil, its title and a short description of the purpose of the Bill which has been prepared by the proposer (usually a Government Minister in the Dáil or the Leader of the Seanad) and accepted by the Ceann Comhairle, appear on a paper known as the Order Paper. The proposing member moves for leave to introduce the Bill to the House. This is known as a motion. If the motion is opposed, the Ceann Comhairle allows both the proposer and opposer to make explanatory statements. Thus, the Ceann Comhairle puts what is known as a question on the motion and the members vote on it. Consequently, if permission is given to introduce the Bill, an order is made for the Bill's consideration on second reading and the Bill is printed.

Second stage

The second stage essentially consists of a debate on the motion confined to the general principle of the Bill. Members may at this second stage raise matters that they feel should be included in the Bill. If the second reading is agreed to, the Bill will then be considered in a committee of either the whole House (the Dáil) or by a special or select committee.

Third stage

This is essentially the committee stage. The Bill is considered section by section in a committee and amendments may be made. Amendments must be relevant and must not be in conflict with the principle of the Bill.

Fourth stage

At this stage the committee reports back and the Bill is considered *in toto*. Amendments may be made but they must not be amendments previously rejected in committee or amendments that involve a charge upon state funds. When amendments have been dealt with, the Bill, or the Bill as amended, is then given a final consideration, following which the Bill proceeds on to the fifth and final stage.

Fifth stage

This fifth and final stage consists of a general debate on the contents of the Bill. Only verbal amendments may be made. A vote is taken on the question that "the Bill do now pass".

On for the position of Seanad Éireann, see below under each individual type of Bill.

When a Bill, other than a Bill to amend the Constitution, has been passed or has been deemed to have been passed by both Houses, it is sent to the President for signature and promulgation into law (see Art.25.1 of the Constitution).

If an Act has no commencement date on it, it is deemed to come into effect when signed into law by the President.

Sometimes an Act will not have a commencement date but it will say words to the effect that it is to come into operation on such day as the Government appoints. In these situations secondary legislation is used to implement the Act and the legal instrument used will contain the commencement date appointed.

ORDINARY BILLS

Ordinary Bills, when passed by the Dáil, are sent to the Seanad. The Seanad has 90 days, or if agreed upon by both Houses, a longer period known as the stated period, in which to consider the Bill. Should it pass without amendment within the stated period, the Bill proceeds to the President. However, if the Bill is amended by the Seanad it returns to the Dáil for its further consideration. Should the Seanad reject the Bill completely or return it to the Dáil with amendments that are unacceptable to that House, the Bill lapses. Such a Bill will not lapse where Dáil Éireann passes a resolution within 180 days after the stated period, declaring that the Bill is deemed to have passed both Houses of the Oireachtas. Thus, the Seanad can only delay rather than prevent the Bill from becoming law if the Dáil wishes otherwise unless the Seanad is successful in invoking the Art.27 of the Constitution procedure.

The Seanad may also initiate an ordinary Bill and in such a case there is no stated period. When passed by the Seanad it goes to the Dáil and, if amended, it is treated as a Bill initiated in the Dáil and the procedure outlined above is followed.

Article 26 reference

The President, after consultation with the Council of State, may refer an Ordinary Bill to the Supreme Court for a decision as to whether all, or any of its provisions, are repugnant to the Constitution. This is known as an Article 26 reference. This is a discretionary power and must be exercised within seven days. Where the Supreme Court decides that the Bill or any part of it is repugnant to the Constitution, the President must decline to sign it and the Bill lapses. Should the Supreme Court find no constitutional objection, the President must sign it as soon as possible after the court's decision is pronounced.

The power of the Irish President to refer bills to the Supreme Court for an advisory opinion under an Article 26 reference is an important and striking feature of the Constitution of 1937. Notwithstanding this, it has been criticised because of the abstract character of proceedings under the reference. Essentially, under the Article 26 reference a putative plaintiff challenges the Bill and a putative defendant defends it. In other words as it has been put, there is "no concrete dispute" between the putative plaintiff and the putative defendant.

If the Supreme Court makes a finding that the Bill is repugnant to the Constitution, the entire Bill, not just any offending provisions fails. In other words, the offending provisions cannot be severed from the Bill which can be unfortunate in that the Bill may otherwise be very worthwhile.

Once a Bill has successfully passed an Article 26 reference it is immune to any future constitutional challenges.

TAXATION BILLS

A Taxation Bill is in effect a Money Bill. The Chairman of Dáil Éireann (An Ceann Chomhairle) certifies a Bill to be a Money Bill. This Bill must be initiated in the Dáil and once passed goes to the Seanad for consideration only. The Seanad may within 21 days make recommendations to the Dáil regarding its contents which the Dáil may accept or reject. The Seanad cannot reject or amend such a Bill. The only power the Seanad has in this case is to challenge the certification of the Chairman of the Dáil that the Bill is a Taxation Bill. To date, the certificate of the Ceann Chomhairle has never been challenged.

ABRIDGED-TIME BILLS

The period of time given to the Seanad to consider a Bill from the Dáil may be abridged by the Dáil at the request of the Taoiseach. This request must also derive from the President after consulting with the Council of State. This arises in circumstances where, in the opinion of the Government, the Bill is urgently and immediately necessary for the preservation of public peace and security or by reason of a public domestic or international emergency. A Bill to amend the Constitution is excluded from the abridged-time Bills procedure.

Bills to amend the Constitution

A proposal to amend the Constitution can only be initiated in the Dáil. Such a Bill cannot contain any other proposal. The progress of such a Bill through the two Houses of the Oireachtas is as outlined above except that such a Bill, instead of proceeding to the President, must be submitted to the people in a referendum for their decision. If a simple majority of the people vote in favour of its enactment, the President, on being satisfied that the provisions of the Constitution in this regard have been complied with, signs and promulgates the Bill as a law.

Consolidation Bills

A Consolidation Bill is a Bill certified by the Attorney General as not containing substantive amendment of the law. A Consolidation Bill may be introduced in either House (usually the Seanad). After receiving a second reading, the Bill is referred to a committee which reports it with or without amendment to the Dáil and the Seanad. The Bill then goes through the fourth and fifth stages in the initiating House and is sent to the other House where the first, second and third stages are waived and it is considered on the fourth and fifth stages only. It is then enacted in the same way as an ordinary bill.

Private Member's Bills

If a member of the Oireachtas other than a minister or Minister of State proposes a Bill it is called a "Private Member's Bill" unless the Government decide to adopt it, which rarely happens. If the Bill passes the second stage, it is referred to a special or select committee. Bills involving a charge on public funds cannot proceed beyond the second stage without the appropriate motion being moved by a member of the Government. Private Member's Bills can be killed off at this stage if they are not approved by the Government. In the Seanad, a Private Member's Bill proceeds in the same way as a Government Bill. The chances of a Private Member's Bill reaching the statute books are remote because even where the Government is in favour, the proposing member is normally requested to withdraw the Bill on the assurance that the Government will introduce a similar measure. A notable exception was the Judicial Separation and Family Law Reform Act 1989 which was first introduced as a Private Member's Bill by Deputy Alan Shatter.

Private Bills

Private Bills are Bills promoted for a particular interest or benefit of a person or locality as distinct from measures of public policy. It is introduced in the

Seanad after an examination by the Examiner of Private Bills. After the second reading has been agreed by the Seanad, the Bill is referred to a joint committee of both Houses who considers the Bill, takes evidence, hears counsel on behalf of the promoters and objectors, considers reports from state departments and reports the Bill with or without amendments to both Houses. The fourth and fifth stages are taken in the Seanad and the Bill is sent to the Dáil where it is considered on fourth and fifth stages only. An example of a Private Bill is The Johnstown Castle Agricultural College Act 1945.

THE INTERPRETATION OF LEGISLATION

INTRODUCTION

The interpretation of legislation or statutory interpretation is the establishing of the meaning, where there is doubt or ambiguity, of a word, phrase, sentence, subsection or section of an Act or statutory instrument. Where there is doubt about the meaning of a statutory provision, it is left to the courts to interpret exactly what the legislature meant when they enacted the provision in question.

In this task of interpretation, the courts are assisted by statutory provisions and by interpretative aids.

The statutory provisions are the Interpretation Act 2005 and the Interpretation (Amendment) Act 1997.

In addition, various Acts have their own interpretation section dealing with various definitions in that Act. This is the first place to be consulted in the interpretative quest.

The interpretative aids are:

- The rules/approaches to interpretation;
- The presumptions; and
- The maxims.

THE INTERPRETATION ACTS

If the statute containing the provision under scrutiny by the court does not itself contain an interpretation section or if the section is of no help then the next port of call is the Interpretation Act 2005 (the "2005 Act") and Interpretation (Amendment) Act 1997. The Interpretation Act 2005 has repealed the previous Interpretation Acts such as the Acts of 1889, 1923, 1937 and 1993.

The Interpretation Act 2005

Section 18 of the 2005 Act contains a number of rules and definitions which are of general application, thus saving the need to specify these matters in each statute individually. For example:

> words which import the singular also include the plural and vice versa unless a contrary intention appears;
>
> a word which imports the masculine should be interpreted as including the feminine unless a contrary intention appears.
>
> the word 'person' includes corporate bodies unless the contrary intention appears.

Section 18 re-enacts s.11 of the Interpretation Act 1937 (the "1937 Act"). Section 18(g) re-enacts the prohibition in s.11(g) of the 1937 Act on the use of marginal notes in statutory interpretation subject to limited exceptions provided in s.7.

The most significant section of the 2005 Act is s.5 which provides:

> In construing a provision of any Act (other than a provision that relates to the imposition of a penal or other sanction)—
> (a) that is obscure or ambiguous, or
> (b) that on a literal interpretation would be absurd or would fail to reflect the plain intention of—
> (i) in the case of an Act [of the Oireachtas], the Oireachtas, or
> (ii) in the case of an Act [continued in force by Article 50 of the Constitution], the parliament concerned,
> the provision shall be given a construction that reflects the plain intention of the Oireachtas or parliament concerned, as the case may be, where that intention can be ascertained from the Act as a whole.

Section 5(2) contains similar provision for statutory instruments. Prior to the enactment of s.5 the courts felt that they could depart from the literal rule and use the teleological or purposive approach if that would give an interpretation that more closely matched or expressed the intention of the legislature. See *Mulcahy v Minister for the Marine,* unreported, High Court, November 11, 1994 where the court said:

> "... that does not preclude the Court from departing from the literal construction of an enactment and adopting in its place a teleological or purposive approach, if that would more faithfully reflect the true legislative intention gathered from the Act as a whole."

Following the enactment of s.5 the courts may only depart from the literal approach where the provision in issue is obscure, ambiguous or absurd, or where it fails to reflect the plain intention of the legislature. This is a narrower or more restricted use of the purposive or teleological approach.

Section 6 provides that when interpreting legislation, a court may make allowances for changes in the law, social conditions, technology, the meaning of words used and other relevant matters.

Section 7 sets out what text of an Act a court may make use of when construing a provision of an Act. For example, can marginal notes be used or not.

Interpretation (Amendment) Act 1997

The sole purpose of this Act is to protect the previous operation of repealed common law rules and any penalties incurred or proceedings brought under them.

THE RULES AND APPROACHES OF STATUTORY INTERPRETATION

The method of interpretation whereby the literal, golden and mischief rules were used has been overtaken and we now refer to approaches rather than rules. These approaches are the literal approach and the schematic or teleological approaches (purposive).

THE RULES

The rules of statutory interpretation, which to a degree are now of historical interest only, are:

- The literal rule;
- The golden rule; and
- The mischief rule—purposive approach.

The literal rule

The literal rule, as its name suggests, required the court to attribute to a word its literal (or ordinary, common place or grammatical sense) meaning. See *Rahill v Brady* [1971] I.R. 69 at 86, where it was held that, "in the absence of some special technical or acquired meaning, the language of a statute should be construed according to the ordinary meaning and in accordance with the rules of grammar".

Thus the literal rule is that the intention of the legislature is to be derived predominantly, if not exclusively, from the words in which it chose to express its commands and in the absence of ambiguity, the courts are obliged to accord a statutory provision its literal meaning even where this might have led to an undesirable effect or unjust result. The judicial role was to interpret that which the legislature had expressed and not remedy any supposed defects in the legislation.

The golden rule

Under this rule the court could give a word or phrase a modified or secondary meaning. A court was permitted to invoke this rule if the literal rule would have led to an absurdity or inconsistency. The idea is that the alternative meaning chosen would be consistent with the smooth working of the system which the statute purports to be regulating and the alternative meaning would bring certainty and clarity to the working of the system. See *Shannon Realties v St Michel (Ville de)* [1924] A.C. 185.

When using this rule a court was not confined to examining the provision in isolation but could look at the long title, the preamble and other provisions in the statute to discern the legislative intention. It was, however, precluded from looking at extrinsic materials. See *Minister for Industry and Commerce v Hales* [1967] I.R. 30.

The golden rule has been given statutory gloss by s.5 of the Interpretation Act 2005.

The mischief rule

This is the oldest of the three rules, being around since the Sixteenth Century. This rule allowed a court to examine pre-existing common law in order to determine the defect or mischief which the statute was designed to remedy. The statute was interpreted in a manner which was sufficient to deal with that defect. This rule was outlined in *Heydon's Case* (1584) 3 Co. Rep. 7a at 7b which set down the following guidelines:

1. What was the common law before the making of the Act?
2. What was the mischief and defect for which the common law did not provide?
3. What remedy the Parliament hath resolved and appointed to cure the disease of the Commonwealth,
4. The true reason of the remedy.

Under this rule the court is required to always take a construction that would suppress the mischief and advance the remedy, and suppress subtle inventions and evasions for the continuance of the mischief.

The approaches

The approaches to statutory interpretation are:

1. The literal approach, and
2. The schematic or teleological approach.

The literal approach

The literal approach approximates to the literal rule.

The literal approach was considered to be the primary principle of construction. See *Cork County Council v Whillock* [1993] 1 I.R. 231 at 237 which states: "it is clear ... that the first rule of construction requires a literal construction must be applied. If there is nothing to modify, alter or qualify the language which the statute contains it must be construed in the ordinary and natural meaning of the words and sentences".

The authoritative statement on the literal approach is in *Inspector of Taxes v Kiernan* [1981] I.R. 117 which acknowledged that the court is not precluded from considering the context in which the words appear. The word under consideration in that case was "cattle" as contained in the Income Tax Acts 1918 and 1967. Did the word cattle include pigs or was it intended to include pigs? The question is when the legislature used the word "cattle" in the Income Tax Act did they intend it to include pigs? Does the mere fact that another Act defined the word broadly require that in the context of the Income Tax Act this broad definition of the word "cattle" should apply? (The Towns Improvement (Ireland) Act 1854 defines the word "cattle" as including "horse, mare, gelding, foal, colt, filly, bull, cow, heifer, ox, calf, ass, mule, ram, ewe, lamb, goat, kid or swine".) Swine obviously encompassed pigs but was it intended in the Acts of 1918 and 1967 that "cattle" should include pigs?

In *Kiernan,* three basic rules of statutory interpretation were approved as follows:

1. First, is the provision directed to the public at large or to a particular class who may be expected to use the word or expression in question in a narrow or extended (broad) way or as a term of art in which case the word should be given its ordinary or colloquial meaning.
2. Secondly, if the word or phrase contained in a penal (criminal) or taxation (financial) statute it should be construed strictly.
3. Thirdly, if the word in question is a simple word which has a widespread and unambiguous currency (a meaning generally given to it) then it should be construed drawing primarily on the judge's own experience of its use.

Dictionaries or other literary sources should be looked at only when alternative meanings, regional usages or such like cast doubt on the ordinary meaning.

The schematic or teleological approach

This approach is used where the literal approach leads to an absurdity, just as the golden rule and mischief rule were used in the past. Using this approach where an absurdity arises, the court may reject the literal interpretation and attribute to the words a secondary, modified meaning which the word or phrase is capable of bearing. In adopting an alternative meaning to the literal meaning the court may examine the provision in its wider statutory context and take into account the perceived defect of the pre-existing law.

The first usage of this approach appears to be in *Frescati Estates Ltd v Walker* [1975] I.R. 177 where the Supreme Court was called on to interpret the word "applicant" in relation to a planning provision in the Local Government (Planning and Development) Act 1963. The defendant submitted that the word should bear its literal meaning: anyone who applies is an applicant. The plaintiffs argued that it should be interpreted in a modified sense to mean a person who applies with the consent of the owner and which interpretation would have excluded the defendant. The plaintiffs were successful despite the Act being silent on the question of owner's consent. The reason for the decision was that if the word were given the literal meaning, any person could apply for permission to land they did not own and without the consent of the owner. The Supreme Court said they found "nothing in the scheme of the Act that would allow interfering, if well-intentioned outsiders to intrude into the rights of those with a legal interest ...".

Nestor v Murphy [1979] I.R. 326 at 330 leaves no doubt but that the courts are using this approach. In this case Henchy J. stated that:

> "In such circumstances [that is where there is an absurdity] we must adopt what has been called a schematic or teleological approach."

This case dealt with s.3 of the Family Home Protection Act 1976. A literal approach to the interpretation of the section would lead to a pointless absurdity. The court in essence said you should give s.3 a construction as would avoid the absurdity and you did this by looking look to see what is the purpose of the Act of 1976 and what the primary aim of s.3(1) is.

Thus, when the teleological or schematic approach is used, a court examines the general purpose and scheme of the statute; in seeking to establish the purpose of the Act the court may look at the long title, the subject matter and the pre-existing law it was designed to alter.

In *McCann Ltd v Ó'Culacháin* [1986] I.R. 196, where the courts were required to decide whether manufacturing included the ripening of bananas, the statutory purpose of the Act was identified and the provision in question was interpreted in a manner consistent with that purpose.

In summary, using the schematic or teleological scheme you:

- Establish the purpose of the Act in question, and
- See if the literal meaning leads to an absurdity; if so, the court may give an alternative meaning but must not give the alternative meaning a wider ambit than is necessary to cure the absurdity.

In effect, the court using the schematic or teleological approach reads words into the provision.

AIDS TO STATUTORY INTERPRETATION

The aids to statutory interpretation are:

(1) Presumptions, and

(2) Maxims.

Repealed provisions and external sources may also aid statutory interpretation.

Presumptions

There are 10 presumptions. Like all presumptions, they may be rebutted by evidence to the contrary.

The presumptions are:

1. The presumption of constitutionality;
2. The presumption of compatibility with EC law;
3. The presumption of compatibility with international law;
4. The presumption that all words bear a meaning;
5. The presumption that a statute should be given an "updated" meaning;
6. The presumption against unclear changes in the law;
7. The presumption that penal statutes be construed strictly;
8. The presumption that revenue statutes be construed strictly;
9. The presumption against retrospective effect; and
10. The presumption against extra-territorial effect.

The presumption of constitutionality

Acts of the Oireachtas are presumed to be constitutional. If there is more than one possible interpretation, one of which is constitutional, the interpretation that is constitutional is the preferred one. Further, if two interpretations are constitutional, the interpretation that favours the validity of the provision in question is to be selected. See *East Donegal Co-operative Livestock Mart Ltd v Attorney General* [1970] I.R. 317.

The presumption of compatibility with EU law

EU Regulations and Directives must be interpreted in a manner that is compatible with the provisions of the EU Treaties (primary legislation). See *Blottner v Bestuur van de Niewe Algemene Bedriifsvereniging* [1977] E.C.R. 1141. Similarly, domestic legislation must be interpreted in conformity with EU law. See *Von Coulson and Kamann v Land Nordrheim-Westfalen* [1984] E.C.R. 1891.

The presumption of compatibility with international law

There is a presumption that the State intended to abide by its obligations under international law. See *Ó'Donhmaill v Merrick* [1984] I.R. 151.

The presumption that all words bear a meaning

This is the presumption that the Oireachtas intended that each word in a statutory provision should have a meaning. See *Cork County Council v Whillock* [1993] 1 I.R. 231.

The presumption that a statute should be given an "updated" meaning

It is difficult and impractical to regularly update legislation and state how it is to be applied in modern times where conditions have sometimes significantly changed from the time when the legislation was enacted. If legislation were to be interpreted with reference to its historical context it could not readily be adapted to suit modern conditions. This presumption seeks to alleviate this difficulty. See *State (O'Connor) v Ó'Caomhanaigh* [1963] I.R. 112.

The presumption against unclear changes in the law

If the law is to be changed, it must be done in a way that is clear whether express or by implication. See *Minister for Industry and Commerce v Hales* [1967] I.R. 50.

The presumption that penal statutes be construed strictly

A penal provision in a statute must be interpreted or construed strictly. Thus, if there is more than one possible interpretation, you choose the interpretation that does not cause the penalty to be extended or a new penalty to be created. See *Frascati Estates Ltd v Walker* [1975] I.R. 177.

The presumption that revenue statutes be construed strictly
A provision creating or causing a charge on State or individual finances must be interpreted strictly. The tax or charge created by a statutory provision must be expressed and must be clear and unambiguous. See *Inspector of Taxes v Kiernan* [1981] I.R. 117.

The presumption against retrospective effect
This presumption is in accordance with Art.15.5 of the Constitution and the rule of law. Article 15.5 declares that the legislature cannot declare Acts to be in breach of the law unless they were in breach at the date of commission. In brief, there is a presumption against retrospective legislation, particularly where the retrospective law creates a penalty or a financial liability. See *Hamilton v Hamilton* [1982] I.R. 466.

The presumption against extra-territorial effect
Sometimes laws can have effect outside the State (extra-territorial effect). However, as a general proposition, there is a presumption that laws made within the State are confined to the geographic area of the State unless there is evidence of a contrary intention. See *Chemical Bank v McCormack* [1983] I.L.R.M. 350.

Maxims

There are four Latin maxims which aid statutory interpretation. These are:

1. *Expressio unius est exclusio alterius;*
2. *Ejusdem generis;*
3. *Noscitur a socii; and*
4. *Generalia specialibus non derogant.*

1. *Expressio unius est exclusio alterius*

To express one thing is to exclude another. In *Kiely v Minister for Social Welfare* [1977] I.R. 267, the court held that because the Social Welfare Insurance Appeals Regulations allowed a written statement to be received in evidence in *specified limited* circumstances, it meant that a written statement could not be received in other circumstances. See also, *Minister for Agriculture & Food v Barry* [2008] I.R. 215.

2. *Ejusdem generis*

Where a general word follows particular and specific words of the same nature as itself, it takes its meaning from them and is presumed to be restricted to the same genus as those words. Thus, in the expression dogs, cats and other animals, *other animals* will be interpreted in light of the preceding specific items and thus an *other animal* will be interpreted as falling into the same category as and to share the characteristics of dogs and cats—that is other domestic animals of some type and would not include animals such as slugs, snails, crocodiles or snakes. See *Cronin v Lunham Brothers Ltd* [1986] I.L.R.M. 415 at 417.

In *People (DPP) v Farrell* [1986] I.R. 258 it was held that, "a Garda Siochana station, a prison or other convenient place" did not include a police car. The court said that other convenient place meant a convenient building of some type.

3. *Noscitur a socii*

A thing is known by its associates or is known by the company it keeps. This rule can also be invoked to give a restricted meaning to otherwise general words. See for example, *Foster v Diphwys Casson* (1887) 18 Q.B.D. 428 where a statutory provision stated that explosives taken into a mine must be in a "case or canister". The defendant used a cloth bag. The courts had to decide whether a cloth bag would fall within the definition of a "case or canister". With the aid of this maxim, it was held that the bag could not have been within the statutory definition because a cloth bag was not a container of the same strength as a case or canister.

4. *Generalia specialibus non derogant*

A statute containing general subject matter is taken not to affect one which applies to a specific topic. The effect of this rule is to prevent the unintentional repeal or qualification of a specific provision by a later one that is of general nature. See *McGonagle v McGonagle* [1951] I.R. 123. See also, *DPP v Grey* [1980] I.R. 317.

European Union Law

Introduction

Ireland became a member of the European Community in 1973. The European Community then comprised three communities:

1. The European Coal and Steel Community (ESCS)
2. The European Atomic Energy Community (EAEC)
3. The European Economic Community (EEC)

The aims of the then European Community was a closer union among the people of Europe and the creation of a common market.

Membership of the EEC initially was in single figures but today the European Union (EU) comprises 27 countries, referred to as Member States.

Every action the European Union can lawfully take is laid down in the various treaties. Based on a treaty provision (art.249), the institutions of the EU can enact legislation which is applicable in all the Member States.

The following are the current Member States of the EU:

- The big five: France, Germany, Spain, Italy, United Kingdom
- The Benelux group: Netherlands, Belgium, Luxembourg
- The Scandinavian group: Denmark, Sweden, Finland
- The smaller outlying states: Ireland, Portugal, Austria, Greece
- The new Member States: Bulgaria, Cyprus, Czech Republic, Estonia, Hungary, Latvia, Lithuania, Malta, Poland, Romania, Slovak Republic and Slovenia.

Some countries have decided to remain outside the EU but instead have become members of the European Economic Area (EEA). Switzerland, though not a member of the EEA, adopts many EU measures and allows free movement of EU citizens. The EEA is an agreement entered into in 1992 between these countries and the Member States of the EC/EU. The Channel Islands, the Isle of Man and Turkey also remain outside the EU but have economic ties with the EU.

European Economic Area (EEA)

Norway, Iceland and Liechtenstein form the EEA. The Member States of the EEA operate a free trade area with the Member States of the EU. Many of the core elements of European Community law apply such as law relating to the Four Freedoms. (See further below at p.54).

European Free Trade Association

The European Free Trade Association (EFTA) is a free trade organisation between four European countries that operates parallel, and is linked to, the European Union (EU). EFTA was established in 1960 by the Stockholm Convention (this Convention was replaced by the Vaduz Convention) a trade bloc alternative for European States who did not join the then EEC. The Convention seeks to provide for the liberalisation of trade among the members.

Initially there were seven member countries: Austria, Denmark, Norway, Portugal, Sweden, Switzerland and the United Kingdom. The current member countries are Iceland, Norway, Lichtenstein and Switzerland.

In 1999 Switzerland concluded a set of bilateral agreements with the European Union covering a wide range of areas, including movement of persons, transport and technical barriers to trade. This development prompted the EFTA States to modernise their Convention to ensure that it will continue to provide a successful framework for the expansion and liberalisation of trade among them and with the rest of the world.

The Institutions of the EU

The main institutions of the European Union are the Council, the Commission, the Parliament, the European Court of Justice, the Court of Auditors, the European Economic and Social Committee, the Committee of the Regions, the European Central Bank and the European Investment Bank.

The Council

This body usually referred to as the European Council was formerly known as the Council of Ministers. Students should not confuse this Council with the Council of Europe which is the institution of the European Convention on Human Rights. The European Council shares with the Commission and the Parliament the responsibility for passing laws and making policy decisions. Notwithstanding the changes brought about by the Lisbon Treaty the Council bears the main responsibility for what the EU does in the field of the common foreign and security policy and for EU action on certain justice issues. The Council consists of ministers from the national governments of all the EU Member States. Meetings are attended by whichever ministers are responsible for the areas under consideration. Thus, for example, if agriculture is the issue under consideration, ministers for agriculture for the various Member States attend.

Most decisions are taken by majority vote, although sensitive issues in areas like taxation, asylum and immigration, or foreign and security policy, *currently* require unanimity.

The Commission

The Commission represents and upholds the interests of Europe as a whole. It is independent of national governments. It drafts proposals for new European laws, which it presents to the European Parliament and the Council. It manages the day-to-day business of implementing EU policies and spending EU funds. The Commission is also guardian of the treaties and laws of the EU. The Commission is empowered to take action against rule-breakers, taking them to the European Court of Justice if necessary. Each Member State has a Commissioner nominated by their national governments. However, the Commissioner is there to represent the EU rather than the national agenda of his/her Member State.

The Parliament

The European Parliament shares responsibility for passing laws with the Council. The Parliament also shares joint responsibility for approving the annual budget of the EU. The Parliament has the power to dismiss the European Commission.

Members of the European Parliament (MEPs) do not sit in national blocks, but in seven Europe-wide political groups. The Parliament is elected every five years. Elections for members of the European Parliament are held in the Member States. The Parliament elects the European Ombudsman, who investigates citizens' complaints regarding maladministration by the EU institutions.

The courts

The European Court of Justice

The European Court of Justice (ECJ) is composed of a judge from each Member State and a number of Advocates General. The judges and Advocates General are nominated by the governments of the Member States for a renewable term of six years from among lawyers whose independence is beyond doubt and who possess the qualifications required for appointment in their respective countries to the highest judicial offices, or who are of recognised competence. The judges of the court elect one of their number as President of the court for a renewable term of three years.

The Advocates General assist the court. They are responsible for presenting, with complete impartiality and independence, an "opinion" in the cases assigned to them.

The Court of First Instance

The Court of First Instance (CFI) was set up to alleviate the work-load of the ECJ. It is made up of at least one judge from each Member State. The judges are appointed by agreement of the Member State governments for a renewable mandate of six years.

Unlike the Court of Justice, the Court of First Instance does not have permanent Advocates General. However, the function of an Advocate General may, in exceptional circumstances, be carried out by a judge.

The jurisdiction of the CFI is limited to hearing appeals from the Commission in competition law cases, and disputes brought by the Commission and the other institutions of the EU relating to staff issues.

There is a right of appeal from this court to the ECJ.

The jurisdiction of the ECJ

The duty of the ECJ is to make sure that EU law is interpreted and applied uniformly in all EU countries. It seeks to ensure, for example, that national courts do not give different rulings on the same issue. The court also seeks to ensure that EU Member States and institutions do what the law requires them to do.

To enable it properly to fulfil its task, the court has been given a clearly defined jurisdiction.

The various types of proceedings that may be taken to the court are actions for:

- Failure to fulfil treaty obligations—art.226 (ex art.169).
- Actions for annulment or review of legality of acts, other than recommendations and opinions adopted by the Commission, Council and the Parliament—art.230 (ex art.173) and art.231 (ex art.174).
- Article 234 (ex art.177) references. This is similar to a case stated procedure by national courts of the Member States. The CFI cannot hear an article 234 reference.

EU Legislation

The legislative product of the EU

The legislative product of the EU consists of treaties, regulations, directives and decisions, all of which are legally binding, except in the case of treaties, provisions that are aspirational in nature.

The EU legal system consistes of primary legislation and secondary legislation. The various treaties are the primary legislation whereas regulations, directives and decisions are secondary legislation. There is a further legal instrument called a recommendation that is not binding.

The treaties

The treaties are a primary source of law. They have been added to and amended. The most recent one, the Treaty of Lisbon establishing a Constitution for Europe, aims to replace all the existing treaties with a single text. The Constitution was adopted by the heads of state and government at the Brussels European Council in June 2004 and was signed in Rome on October 29, 2004. The Lisbon Treaty was signed by the Member States on December 13, 2007 and entered into force on December 1, 2009.

Students should note that following the Treaty Of Amsterdam (TOA) the treaty articles were renumbered, and should be aware when reading judgments of the European Court of Justice and the Commission prior to the TOA that the treaty articles will be referred to by their old numbers.

The provisions or articles of the treaties may be capable of direct effect and are legally binding except, as already noted, where they are of an aspirational nature only.

The following are the various treaties:

- Treaty establishing the European Coal and Steel Community;
- Treaty of Rome;
- Merger Treaty;
- Single European Act (SEA);
- Treaty on the European Union (Maastricht Treaty—TEU);
- Treaty of Amsterdam;
- Treaty of Nice; and
- The Lisbon Treaty.

The Treaty establishing the European Coal and Steel Community (ECSC)

This Treaty was signed on April 18, 1951 in Paris and entered into force on July 23, 1952. This Treaty expired on July 23, 2002.

The Treaty of Rome

This Treaty which was signed in Rome on March 25, 1957 and entered into force on January 1, 1958, established the European Economic Community (EEC) and the European Atomic Energy Community (Euratom), and the two are jointly known as the Treaties of Rome.

The Merger Treaty

This Treaty, which provided for a Single Commission and a Single Council of the then three European Communities was signed in Brussels on April 8, 1965 and entered into force on July 1, 1967.

The Single European Act (SEA)

This Treaty was signed in Luxembourg and in the Hague, and entered into force on July 1, 1987. It provided for the adaptations required for the achievement of the internal market.

The Treaty on the European Union

This Treaty, which is often referred to as the Maastricht Treaty, was signed in Maastricht on February 7, 1992 and entered into force on November 1, 1993. The Maastricht Treaty changed the name of the European Economic Community to simply "the European Community". It also introduced new forms of co-operation between the Member State governments, for example, on defence and in the area of "justice and home affairs". By adding this inter-governmental co-operation to the existing "Community" system, the Maastricht Treaty created a new structure with three "pillars" (discussed further below at p.55).

The Treaty of Amsterdam

The Treaty of Amsterdam was signed on October 2, 1997 and entered into force on May 1, 1999. It amended and renumbered the treaty articles. Consolidated versions of the EU and EC treaties are attached to it.

The Treaty of Nice

The Treaty of Nice was signed on February 26, 2001 and entered into force on February 1, 2003. It deals, in the main, with reforming the institutions so that the Union may function efficiently after its enlargement with the addition of new Member States. The Treaty of Nice, the former Treaty of the EU and the Treaty of the EC have been merged into one consolidated version.

The Lisbon Treaty

The stated purpose of the Lisbon or Reform Treaty is to enhance "the efficiency and democratic legitimacy of the Union" and to improve its coherence. The Treaty will provide the EU with modern institutions, altering the structure of them and how they work. The Treaty of Lisbon will reinforce democracy in the EU and its capacity to promote the interests of its citizens on a day-to-day basis.

Regulations, directives, decisions and recommendations

Article 249 EC (ex art.189) of the Treaty of Rome is the foundational provision as regards the creation of legal instruments. This article empowers the institutions of the European Community and the Union to approve legally binding instruments in order to implement the general principles contained in the Treaties. Three types of legally binding instruments are provided for in this article. As already noted, these are:

- Regulations;
- Directives; and
- Decisions.

There is also a recommendation which, as already noted, is not legally binding but is highly persuasive.

1. Regulations

Article 249 of the EC Treaty states as follows:

> A Regulation shall have general application. It shall be binding in its entirety and directly applicable in all Member States.

Thus, regulations are addressed to *all* Member States.

In accordance with the decision of the European Court of Justice in a triology of cases, once a regulation is made in accordance with the powers conferred by the treaty it automatically becomes law in all Member States. See *Van Gend en Loos v Nederlandse Belastingenadministratie* [1963] E.C.R. 1; *Costa v ENEL* [1964] E.C.R. 585; and *Internationale Handelsgesellschaft v Einfuhr and Vorratsstelle fur Getreide und Futtermittel* [1970] E.C.R. 1125.

Regulations are capable of direct effect. A regulation is an appropriate legislative vehicle where the matter covered by the regulation does not overlap with any existing national laws of the Member States.

2. *Directives*

Article 249 (ex art.189) of the Treaty states as follows:

> A Directive shall be binding as to the result to be achieved, upon each Member State to which it is addressed, but shall leave to the national authorities the choice of form and methods.

There is, however, a special provision in a directive called a derogation that allows it to be applied in appropriate cases in different ways. A derogation is not an exemption. It usually just permits greater flexibility in the application of the law to take into account special circumstances.

Sometimes a directive will have a time limit within which the Member State must implement the directive. Subsequently, the directive is directly applicable and capable of direct effect and may be relied on in national courts of the Member States. In order for a directive to be directly applicable and to have a direct effect three conditions must be satisfied. See further at p.52.

3. *Decisions*

A decision is binding on the Member State to which it is addressed. It is the legal instrument used when it is to apply to one or only some Member States. Article 249 of the Treaty provides:

> A Decision shall be binding in its entirety upon those to whom it is addressed.

4. *Recommendations*

Recommendations and opinions need not be implemented because they are not binding, but nonetheless are of persuasive value. Article 249 states that:

> Recommendations and Opinions shall have no binding force.

THE LEGISLATIVE PROCESS

The treaties provide for four main legislative processes. These are:

1. The "Consultation" procedure.
2. The "Assent" procedure.
3. The "Co-Decision" procedure.
4. The "Co-Operation" procedure.

Every proposal for a new European law is based on a specific treaty article, referred to as the "legal basis", which lays down which of the above four processes or procedures are to be used for that particular proposal.

It is the Commission who initiates the law-making procedure by presenting a proposal.

The voting system will either be unanimity voting, qualified majority voting, double majority voting, reinforced majority voting or Ioannina compromise.

1. The Consultation procedure

Under this procedure the Council consults Parliament as well as the European Economic and Social Committee (EESC) and the Committee of the Regions (CoR)—the Council then submits the Commission proposal to the Parliament. The Parliament has three options:

- approve the Commission proposal.
- reject the Commission proposal.
- ask for amendments to the Commission proposal.

In this procedure, as in all the others, if the Council amends a Commission proposal it must do so unanimously.

2. The Assent procedure

Here the Council must obtain the Parliament's assent before certain important decisions are taken. The procedure is the same as the "Consultation" procedure except that the Parliament cannot amend the proposal under this procedure. Here its options are:

- accept the proposal;
- reject the proposal.

3. The Co-Decision procedure

Here the Parliament does not merely give its opinion, it shares legislative power equally with the Council. If Council and Parliament cannot agree on a piece of proposed legislation it is put to a conciliation committee composed of equal numbers of Council and Parliament representatives. Once this committee has reached an agreement the text is sent once again to the Parliament and the Council so that they can finally adopt it as law. This is the procedure that is most frequently used.

4. The Co-Operation procedure

Here the Commission and Council act in co-operation with the Parliament. A common position is adopted by the Council and it goes to the Parliament for consideration. If within three months the Parliament amends the common position, the Commission must within a further month review the Parliament's amendments and may revise its proposal. In this case the Council, within a further three months may adopt the Commission's revised proposal (if necessary) by qualified majority voting (QMV). However, it may adopt the Parliament's amendments that were not approved by the Commission or otherwise amend the Commission's revised proposal, in which cases the Council would be required to vote unanimously (unanimity); or it may fail to act, in which case the Commission proposal lapses. If, however, within three months of the common position, the Parliament either approves the common position or takes no position on it, then the Council adopts the directive.

The Nature of EU Law

Introduction

When considering the nature of EU law, three issues fall for consideration. These are the incorporation of EU law into the Irish legal system; the supremacy of EU law over the domestic law of the individual Member States; and the capability of EU law for direct effect in the Member States.

In *Van Gend en Loos* the court put the nature of EEC law, as it then was, thus:

> "... [T]he Community constitutes a new legal order of international law, for the benefit of which the States have limited their sovereign rights, albeit within limited fields, and the subjects of which comprise not only Member States but also their nationals. Independently of the legislation of Member States, Community law therefore not only imposes obligations on individuals but is also intended to confer upon them rights which become part of their legal heritage. These rights arise not only where they are expressly granted by the Treaty, but also by reason of obligations which the Treaty imposes in a clearly defined way upon individuals as well as upon Member States and upon the institutions of the Community."

The nature of EU law can be summed up thus: EU law is supreme; EU law may be directly applicable in the Member States and may be capable of direct effect.

The incorporation of EU law into the Irish legal system

EU law may be directly applicable; this means that no domestic implementing legislation is necessary in order for its incorporation into Irish law. Students should not confuse direct applicability with the doctrine of direct effect. (On direct effect, see further below at p.52).

Article 15.2.1° of the Constitution provides that only the Oireachtas may make laws for the State. The fact that the laws of the EU are capable of being incorporated into the Irish legal system, without the need for domestic implementing legislation, is clearly in conflict with Art.15.2.1°. Article 29.5.6° of the Constitution, which allows for the incorporation into Irish law of laws made outside Ireland, could not resolve this conflict because this Article provides that in order for international treaties to be incorporated into domestic law, an implementing Act of the Oireachtas is necessary.

To overcome difficulties with the incorporation of EU law into Irish law Art.29.4.10° was inserted into the Constitution following a referendum and the European Communities Act 1972 was enacted by the Oireachtas.

In *Crotty v An Taoiseach* [1987] I.R. 713, further amendments were made to Art.29.4, again following a referendum, in order for the Government to ratify the Single European Act. In *Crotty* it was held that the effects of Art.29.4.10° were far reaching and that the Constitution "could not now be invoked to invalidate any measure which the State was directed by the institutions of the European Communities to take". The institutions referred to in *Crotty* expressly included the ECJ.

Article 29.4.10° provides:

> No provision of this Constitution invalidates laws enacted, acts done or measures adopted by the State which are necessitated by the obligations of membership of the European Union or of the Communities, or prevents laws enacted, acts done or measures adopted by the European Union or by the Communities or by institutions thereof, or by bodies competent under the Treaties establishing the Communities from having the force of law in the State.

Although the effect of Art.29.4.10° was that EU law became part of Irish law, Art.29.4.10° has not been without its difficulties. For example, what did the word "necessitated" in Art.29.4.10° encompass. The courts held that "necessitated" included acts consequent upon Ireland's membership of the EU (see *Lawlor v Minister for Agriculture* [1990] I.R. 356). The courts have also held that if an action is so far reaching or so detached from the result to be achieved by a particular EU law, it is not necessitated (see *Greene v Minister for Agriculture* [1990] 2 I.R. 17).

Supremacy of EU Law

EU law is supreme over the national law of the individual Member States. This notion of supremacy binds all organs of the State, legislature, executive and judiciary alike. It matters not whether the EU provisions in question all contained in a treaty, a regulation, a directive or decision; nor does it matter if the conflicting national provision is contained in a constitution, in legislation or other legal instrument.

If it were otherwise, Member States might apply EU law differently or might not apply it at all. Thus the supremacy of EU law ensures uniformity of application by the individual Member States and helps bring about the aim of closer European integration.

The concept of the supremacy of EU law is not set out expressly in the treaties, but in the trilogy of cases beginning with *Van Gend en Loos v Nederlandse Belastingenadministratie* [1963] E.C.R. 1; *Costa v ENEL* [1964] E.C.R. 585; and *Internationale Handelsgesellschaft v Einfuhr and Vorratsstelle fur Getreide und Futtermittel* [1970] E.C.R. 1125, the ECJ held that EEC law was supreme.

The supremacy of EU law was well settled by the time Ireland became a member in 1973.

As a result of the doctrine of supremacy, a national court called upon to apply provisions of EU law must give full effect to those provisions and must, if necessary, refuse to apply any conflicting provisions of national law. The court is not required to wait until the offending provision is set aside by other means such as by legislative or constitutional means. See *Simmenthal SpA* (C–106/77) [1978] E.C.R. 629. This principle applies in both civil and criminal law. See *Procureur du Roi v Dassonville* [1974] E.C.R. 837.

The doctrine of direct effect

The phrase "direct effect" means that provisions of EU law which give individuals of Member States rights or impose obligations may be enforced in the national courts of Member States.

The provisions of the treaties, regulations and directives are capable of direct effect provided the following three step test is satisfied:

1. the provision in question must be clear and precise;
2. it must be unconditional;
3. it must be such that no further action is required by the Community institutions or by the Member States or, if the provision requires the Member States to amend their laws, it leaves no discretion to the Member States about the content of those amendments.

The above test was first referred to in *Van Gend En Loos v Nederlandse Administratie der Belastingen* (C–26/62) [1963] E.C.R. 1 but was set out more explicitly, in the above three step formula, in *Reyners v Belgium* [1974] E.C.R. 631.

Direct effect can be what is known as:

- Vertical direct effect, or
- Horizontal direct effect.

Vertical direct effect is where an individual of a Member State can rely on a provision of EU law to assert rights against a Member State in that Member State's national court. Horizontal direct effect, which applies only to treaty provisions and regulations, is where an individual of a Member State can rely on a provision of EU law to assert rights based on EU law against another individual before a court of a Member State. See *Defrenne v SABENA* (No.2) (C–43/75) [1976] E.C.R. 455.

Treaties and direct effect

Treaty provisions are capable of direct effect (*Van Gend en Loos*). However, in order to have direct effect and be legally enforceable in a Member State, the three step test, noted above, must be satisfied.

Treaty provisions may have vertical direct effect or horizontal direct effect. For a while after *Van Gend en Loos* it was assumed that only treaty provisions which were prohibitive in nature were capable of direct effect. However, this is not the case. In *Alfons Lutticke GmbH v Hauptzollamt Saarloouis* [1966] E.C.R. 205, the ECJ said that treaty provisions that were positive in nature were also capable of direct effect once any time limit set in the article had expired.

Regulations and direct effect

Provisions of regulations may have vertical direct effect or horizontal direct effect.

Regulations do not generally require implementing legislation in the Member States and will only be appropriate in situations where the above three step test is satisfied. See *Leonesio v Ministero dell'Agricolura delle Foreste* (C–93/71) [1972] E.C.R. 287.

Directives and direct effect

Directives have been held to be capable of direct effect. See *Van Duyn v Home Office* (C–41/74) [1974] E.C.R. 1337.

Directives will only have direct effect when the above three step test is satisfied. Further, in the case of directives the timeframe for the implementation of the directive must have expired. See *Pubblico Ministero v Ratti* [1979] E.C.R. 1629.

Provisions of directives are not capable of horizontal direct effect. See *Marshall v Southampton and South West Hampshire Area Health Authority (Teaching) (No.1)* (C–152/84) [1986] E.C.R. 723.

To the above may be added the decision in *Francovitch v Italian Republic* [1991] E.C.R. I–5357 where the ECJ said that individuals may claim damages from a defaulting state in that state's own national courts where they suffer loss due to state failure to implement EU law. For an Irish case on this issue, see also *Tate v Minister for Social Welfare* [1995] I.R. 419, where the Irish High Court found the State liable for failure to implement the directive on equal treatment for men and women in social security payments.

PRINCIPLES AND CONCEPTS OF EU LAW

THE FOUR FREEDOMS

The phrase "four freedoms" refers to the free movement of goods, persons, services and capital. This phrase succinctly sums up the objectives of the Community and it is part of the substantive law of the EU. See art.3(c) and art.14 (ex art.7a) of the EC Treaty which provides:

> The internal market shall comprise an area without internal frontiers in which the free movement of goods, persons, services and capital is ensured ...

The EU is concerned with what it refers to as "obstacles" to the four freedoms and obstacles to these freedoms are in effect obstacles to the aim of the creation of a closer union between the people of Europe and the creation of a common market.

1. Free movement of goods

Articles 28 and 29 of the Treaty of Rome deal with and prohibit obstacles to the free movement of goods. Obstacles to free movement of goods are quantitative restrictions and measures equivalent to quantitative restrictions (MEQRs). The former are direct restrictions and the latter indirect restrictions. Examples of direct restrictions are quotas imposed by Member States on goods imported into a state, customs duties, import taxes and tariffs. Examples of indirect restrictions are imposing unnecessary criteria regarding technical standards.

Some restrictions or obstacles will be tolerated where it can be shown that they have been imposed, not to restrict the free movement of goods, but rather have been imposed in the interest of public health, public morality, public security or the protection of the environment (art.30).

2. Free movement of workers

Obstacles to free movement of workers (persons) include restrictions on numbers of foreign workers allowed to enter the workforce of a Member State and non-recognition of qualifications of foreign workers. Many judgments have been given in the field of freedom of movement of persons. Certain rights are also given to the families of the workers. A worker includes a person seeking work.

3. Free movement of services

Obstacles to free movement of services (freedom of establishment) come in the form of Member States imposing severe restrictions on the establishment and operation of services, particularly in sectors such as provision of water, electricity, transport and telecommunication, which in most Member States were operated under a state monopoly.

4. Free movement of capital

Obstacles to free movement of capital come in the form of Member States operating exchange control laws that in effect restrict free movement of capital, by restricting the amount of money that could be invested outside that Member State, and also limiting the amount of money that people travelling outside the Member State could take with them.

THE THREE PILLARS

Another phrase referred to in EU law is the "Three Pillars". This phrase comes from an analogy with a Greek temple supported by pillars. The EU is said to be based on Three Pillars, viz.:

Pillar 1. The treaties establishing the ECSC, the EAEC and the EC.

Pillar 2. Common foreign and Security Policy (CFSP).

Pillar 3. Co-operation on judicial and home affairs

Politically all three pillars carry equal weight but legally the first pillar carried most weight because the first pillar is based on the treaties which are legally binding.

THE "*ACQUIS COMMUNAUTAIRE*"

The phrase "*acquis communautaire*" means the legal principles established by the three original treaties, as amended by the Single European Act and the Treaty on the European Union.

THE PRINCIPLE OF SUBSIDIARITY

The principle of subsidiarity means that decisions of the EU must be taken as closely as possible to the citizens of the Member States. Essentially the EU should not take action, except on matters for which it alone is responsible, unless it is more effective than action taken at national, regional or local level.

International Law

INTRODUCTION

A consideration of the Irish legal system involves a consideration of international law.

International law may be public international law or private international law. Public international law governs relationships between states rather than between individuals, whereas private international law deals with relationships between individuals or corporate entities, governing such matters as which country has jurisdiction to decide disputes between parties residing in different jurisdictions.

It is public international law that is under discussion in this Chapter.

International law, as already noted, is that body of law which governs states in their relationships with each other. Thus, the subjects of international law are states (sovereign territorial entities).

International law is composed of rules, and despite the absence of any superior authority to enforce these rules, they are nonetheless considered by states to be binding upon them. It is this fact that gives these rules the status of law. Where a state wishes to avoid a particular rule, it will not argue that international law does not exist, but rather will argue that states have not agreed that a particular rule is to be binding upon them, or that the rule does not apply to the particular situation.

International law operates on the basis that states *consent* to be bound. A state consents to be bound by international agreements and treaties by one of three means: viz. ratification, signature or accession.

1. Ratification (acceptance, approval or notification) of the completion of procedures required for entry into force of an agreement (where the agreement has first been signed on behalf of the state). States that are part of the agreement at the time of enactment will generally ratify it.

2. Signature (but only where this is done without reservation).

3. Accession (in the case of a multilateral agreement that has not first been signed by or on behalf of the state). Accession applies to states that become party to an agreement after it has been enacted.

prisijungimas prie tarptautinės sutarties

Once a treaty, convention, covenant or protocol is adopted by the sponsoring body of the relevant international organisation it is open for signature. As a general rule, a state may sign a treaty without being bound by it, though signing it is often interpreted as commitment in principle to future ratification.

Ratification and accession are effectively the same thing, save that a state accedes to or adheres to a treaty when it did not take part in the negotiation leading to its adoption, but becomes a party afterwards at the invitation of the negotiating states. In practice, the terms ratification and accession are often used interchangeably. Once a state has acceded to or ratifies a treaty it is obliged under international law to abide by the terms of that treaty.

Upon consenting to be bound by a treaty the state becomes a *contracting state*, whether or not that treaty has entered into force. It becomes a party to the treaty only when the treaty has the force of law in that state.

Enforcement mechanisms for breach of international law obligations are different from those that would apply where there is a breach of the rules of national or domestic law. States that do not comply with their international law obligations will be looked upon unfavourably and in some instances may have sanctions, such as trade sanctions or fines, imposed against them.

States that have consented to the compulsory jurisdiction of the International Court of Justice (ICJ) may also find themselves before that court for breaches of international law.

The latin maxim or principle of *pacta sunt servanta* which means that agreements are meant to be kept or carried out in good faith is one of the most important principles underpinning international law. It is enshrined in art.2(2) of the UN Charter. In the *Nuclear Tests* case [1974] I.C.J. Reports 253; 57 I.L.R. 605, the ICJ said "one of the basic principles governing the creation and performance of legal obligations, whatever their source, is the principle of good faith" and just "as the very rule of *pacta sunt servanta* in the law of treaties is based on good faith, so also is the binding character of international obligations assumed by unilateral obligation".

Article 29.3 of the Irish Constitution provides that, "Ireland accepts the generally recognised principles of international law as its rule of conduct in its relations with other States".

Sources of International Law

The main or primary sources of international law are the various international treaties, agreements, conventions and covenants themselves, custom and practice (state practice), general principles of law recognised by civilised nations and the case law of the International Court of Justice. Judicial decisions and teachings of the most highly qualified publicists of the various nations provide a secondary source.

Article 38 of the statute of the ICJ expressly directs the ICJ to apply the above sources of law in deciding disputes.

Decisions of a national court may also amount to a statement of what the ICJ considers to be international law on a particular matter. Such a decision would only carry weight as evidence of international law where the court is of very high standing and where the international law issue was central to the case and received careful consideration. See, for example, important decisions of the United States Supreme Court in the *Paquete Habana* case (175 US 677 (1900)) and the House of Lords *In Re Pinochet* [1999] UKHL 52. See also, *The Lotus* (PCIJ Series A, No. 10, 1927, p.18; 4 I.L.R. 153) where the predecessor of the ICJ examined decisions of French national courts in order to discover what the State practice of France was on the subject in issue.

For an Irish perspective see the decision of Irish Supreme Court in *Government of Canada v The Employment Appeals Tribunal and Burke* [1992] 2 I.R. 494.

The Incorporation of International Law

There are two mechanisms by which states incorporate international law into their own legal system. These are the monist approach and the dualist approach. Ireland operates a dualist system.

Whether a state operates a monist or dualist system it is rarely necessary for the terms of an international agreement to be incorporated into domestic law in order for the state to be bound by that agreement and to fulfil the obligations it assumes under it. However, a national court will not be obliged to enforce the obligations under an agreement unless that agreement has been expressly incorporated into domestic law of the state in question. In other words the provisions of an unincorporated international agreement cannot be relied upon in a national court. See, for example, *In Re O'Laighleis* [1960] I.R. 93.

Monist approach

Where a state uses a monist approach (monism), as soon as that state has signed up to an international agreement it becomes law in that state without the need for any further legislative action by that state.

Dualist approach

Where a state uses a dualist approach (dualism), although that state has signed up to an international agreement the agreement does not have the force of law in that state until the state has enacted implementing legislation. In other words, a domestic Act must be enacted by the legislature of the particular state. For example, Ireland signed up to and ratified the European Convention of Human Rights on February 26, 1953 but it was only incorporated into domestic law when the Oireachtas enacted the European Convention of Human Rights Act 2003. Thus, prior to that date it could not be relied on in the Irish courts. See *Norris v Attorney General* [1984] I.R. 36.

Ireland and International Law

Ireland is party to many international agreements, conventions, covenants and treaties.

Entering into an international agreement is a significant measure that impacts upon Ireland's legal obligations and its relations with other states. Article 29 of the Constitution sets down a number of substantial and procedural requirements that must be strictly followed whenever an international agreement is being concluded.

Article 29.4.1° of the Constitution provides that, "the executive power of the State in or in connection with its external relations shall be exercised by or on the authority of the Government".

Article 29.5.1° provides that, "every international agreement to which the State becomes a party must be laid before Dáil Éireann".

Article 29.5.2° provides that if any international agreement imposes a charge on public funds that are not of a technical and administrative character that agreement must be approved by Dáil Éireann prior to the Government agreeing to the State being bound by it.

Article 29.6 provides that, "no international agreement shall be part of domestic law of the State save as may be determined by the Oireachtas".

Incorporation of International Law into the Irish Legal System

As previous mentioned, Ireland adopts a dualist approach to the incorporation of international law which means that the terms of an international agreement do not become part of the domestic law of the State unless expressly incorporated by an Act of the Oireachtas in accordance with Art.29.6.

However, even without express incorporation into domestic law, international law might prove to be influential because of Art.29.1–Art.29.3 of the Constitution, which provides that the State accepts the generally recognised principles of international law in its relation with other states. Thus the provisions in Arts 29.1, 29.2 and 29.3 are capable of being invoked in our national courts. In relation to Art.29.1 and Art.29.2, to date there has been only one judicial reference. See *McGimpsey v Ireland* [1990] 1 I.R. 110. On the other hand, Art.29.3 has provided the legal basis for a number of challenges to legislation, particularly regarding extradition. These challenges invariably were without success. See, for example, *State (Duggan) v Tapley* [1952] I.R. 52; and *State (Quinn) v Ryan* [1965] I.R. 70; and *Magee v Culligan* [1992] 1 I.R. 223.

The nature and effect of Ireland entering into international law treaties and agreements and their relationship with national laws was discussed in *In re O'Laighleis* [1960] I.R. 93 where the court could not accept the idea that the primacy of domestic legislation is displaced by the State becoming a party to a Convention because Art.15.2.1° of the Constitution had given the sole and exclusive power to make laws for the State to the Oireachtas and no other legislative authority has power to make laws for the State and because Art.29.6 provided that "no international agreement shall be part of the domestic law of the State save as may be determined by the Oireachtas". See also *Norris v Ireland* [1984] I.R. 36.

Whereas the cases of *O'Laighleis* and *Norris* continue to represent an accurate statement of the law, the courts have sometimes referred to international conventions as aids to interpreting provisions of Irish law. See, for example, *Crotty v An Taoiseach* [1987] I.R. 713 where the Vienna Convention on the Law of Treaties 1969 was stated by the court to reflect the relevant principles concerning the ratification of treaties even though Ireland had not ratified that Treaty.

Similarly, case law of international courts, such as the International Court of Justice or the European Court of Human Rights, may prove influential notwithstanding the views expressed in *O'Laighleis*. See, for example *Desmond v Glackin (No.2)* [1993] 2 I.R. 67, a case dealing with contempt of court against a government minister and where the court appeared favourably disposed towards the decision in *Irish Times Newspapers Ltd v United Kingdom* (1979 E.H.R.R. 245), a decision of the European Court of Human Rights.

Ireland and International Organisations

Ireland is an active participant in many international organisations such as the United Nations (UN), the Council of Europe and the World Trade Organisation (WTO). Ireland also actively participates in the Organisation for Security and Co-operation in Europe (OSCE) and the Organisation for Economic Co-operation and Development (OECD). Ireland maintains a policy of military neutrality and is not a member of North Atlantic Treaty Organisation (NATO) or any other military alliance. However, for almost 50 years Ireland has been an active contributor to UN and UN-mandated peace-keeping operations.

THE COUNCIL OF EUROPE

Introduction

The Council of Europe is distinct from the European Union. It is based in Strasbourg (France) and is Europe's oldest international political organisation. Founded on May 5, 1949, it now covers virtually the entire European Continent, having 47 member countries. The Council has also granted observer status to five other States (the Holy See, the United States, Canada, Japan and Mexico).

The Council of Europe seeks to develop throughout Europe, common and democratic principles based on the European Convention on Human Rights and other reference texts on the protection of individuals. The Convention was incorporated into Irish law by the enactment of the European Convention of Human Rights Act 2003. Many of the rights protected by the Convention are also protected by the Irish Constitution.

THE STRUCTURE OF THE COUNCIL OF EUROPE

The Council of Europe consists of the Committee of Ministers, the Parliamentary Assembly, the Congress of Local and Regional Authorities, the European Court of Human Rights, the Commissioner for Human Rights, the Conference of INGOs, a Secretary General, a Deputy Secretary General and a Secretariat. The Council has two official languages, English and French. German, Italian and Russian are also working languages.

The Committee of Ministers

This is the Council's decision-making body and is made up of the ministers of foreign affairs of each Member State or their permanent diplomatic representatives in Strasbourg. The Committee of Ministers decides Council of Europe policy and approves its budget and programme of activities.

The Parliamentary Assembly (PACE)

This is the deliberative body and the driving force of the Council of Europe. Its members are appointed by the national parliament of each Member State.

The Congress of Local and Regional Authorities

The Congress is the voice of Europe's regions and municipalities and provides a forum where elected representatives can discuss common problems, pool their experiences and develop policies.

The European Court of Human Rights

This is the permanent judicial body set up under the European Convention on Human Rights and which guarantees for all Europeans the rights safeguarded by the Convention. It is open to states and individuals regardless of nationality. In essence, the court is the enforcement body of the rights guaranteed by the Convention.

Any person who feels his or her rights have been violated under the Convention by a state party can take a case to the court. The decisions of the court are not automatically legally binding, but the court does have the power to award damages. State parties can also take cases against other state parties to the court, although this power is rarely used.

The Commissioner for Human Rights

The Commissioner is an independent body responsible for promoting education, awareness and respect for human rights in Member States. The Commissioner essentially plays a preventive role.

The Conference of INGOs

The Conference includes a vast number of International Non Governmental Organisations (INGOs). It provides vital links between politicians and the public and brings the voice of civil society to the Council. The Council's work benefits extensively from the INGOs, expertise and their outreach to European citizens.

The Secretary General

The Secretary General is at the head of the organisation and is responsible for the strategic planning and direction of the Council's work programme and budget, and oversees the day-to-day management of the organisation. The Secretary General is elected by the Parliamentary Assembly for a five-year term.

The Deputy Secretary General

The Deputy Secretary General is also elected for a five-year term by the Parliamentary Assembly, in an election separate to the one held for the Secretary General.

The Secretariat

In excess of 2,000 permanent staff, from the various Member States, work for the Council of Europe mainly in Strasbourg, but also in other offices throughout Europe assisted by temporary employees.

THE EUROPEAN CONVENTION ON HUMAN RIGHTS (ECHR)

The European Convention on Human Rights (formally the Convention for the Protection of Human Rights and Fundamental Freedoms) is the most important Treaty or Convention of the Council of Europe. It is an international treaty to protect human rights and fundamental freedoms in Europe. The Convention was drafted in1950 by the then, newly formed, Council of Europe. The Convention was opened for signature on November 4, 1950 in Rome. The Convention entered into force on September 3, 1953. All Council of Europe Member States are party to the Convention and new members are expected to ratify the convention at the earliest opportunity.

The Convention established the European Court of Human Rights.

The Convention sets out in a series of articles and protocols the rights protected.

Articles

Article 1, which is the main article, simply binds the signatory parties to secure the rights under the other articles of the Convention within their jurisdiction. In exceptional cases, jurisdiction may not be confined to a contracting state's own national territory.

Article 2 protects the right of every person to their life.

Article 3 prohibits torture and inhuman or degrading treatment or punishment.

Article 4 prohibits slavery, servitude and forced labour.

Article 5 provides that every person has the right to liberty and security of person.

Article 6 provides a detailed right to a fair trial.

Article 7 prohibits the retrospective criminalisation of acts and omissions. This Article incorporates the legal principle *nullum crimen, nulla poena sine lege* (no crime, no punishment without a previous penal law) into the Convention.

Article 8 provides a right to respect for one's private and family life, his home and his correspondence, subject to certain restrictions.

Article 9 provides a right to freedom of thought, conscience and religion.

Article 10 provides the right to freedom of expression, subject to certain restrictions.

Article 11 protects the right to freedom of assembly and association.

Article 12 provides a right for women and men of marriageable age to marry and establish a family. The court has so far refused to apply the protections of this article to same-sex marriage.

Article 13 provides for the right for an effective remedy before national authorities for violations of rights under the Convention.

Article 14 contains a prohibition of discrimination.

Article 15 allows contracting states to derogate from certain rights guaranteed by the Convention in time of war or other public emergency threatening the life of the nation provided three substantive conditions are satisfied.

Article 16 allows states to restrict the political activity of foreigners.

Article 17 has a provision regarding abuse of rights

Article 18 provides that any limitations on the rights provided for in the Convention may be used only for the purpose for which they are provided.

Protocols

As of January 2010, 15 protocols to the Convention have been opened for signature. These can be divided into two main groups, procedural and substantive. The procedural protocols are those changing the machinery of the Convention, whereas the substantive protocols are those adding additional rights to those protected by the Convention.

The substantive protocols protect:

- property rights;
- educational rights;
- the right to regular, free and fair elections;
- the prohibition on the imprisonment of people for breach of a contract;
- the right to freely move within a country once lawfully there and for a right to leave any country;
- the prohibition on the expulsion of nationals and the right of an individual to enter a country of his or her nationality;
- the prohibition on the collective expulsion of foreigners;
- the restriction on the application of the death penalty to times of war or imminent threat of war, the complete abolition of the death penalty;
- the right to fair procedures for lawfully resident foreigners facing expulsion;
- the right to appeal in criminal matters and a right to compensation for the victims of miscarriages of justice, the prohibition on a retrial of a person finally acquitted or convicted of a particular offence (the double jeopardy rule); and the right of equality between spouses.

The procedural protocols, in particular protocols 11 and 14 established a fundamental change in the machinery of the Convention. Individuals may now apply directly to the court, which has been given compulsory jurisdiction. Previously, states could ratify the Convention without accepting the jurisdiction of the Court of Human Rights (protocol 11).

Protocol 14 seeks to "filter" out cases that have less chance of succeeding along with those that are broadly similar to cases brought previously against the same Member State. Furthermore, a case will not be considered admissible where an applicant has not suffered a "significant disadvantage".

A new mechanism was introduced by protocol 14 to assist enforcement of judgments by the Committee of Ministers.

THE UNITED NATIONS

The United Nations (UN), was established at the San Francisco Conference in 1945. The founding instrument of the United Nations is the UN Charter. The purpose of the UN is to maintain international peace and security, and to that end to take effective collective measures for the prevention and removal of threats to the peace and settlement of international disputes or situations which might lead to a breach of the peace (art.1 of the Charter).

The United Nations has been a cornerstone of Irish foreign policy since it joined the organisation on December 14, 1955. For many years, prior to our accession to the European Community, our membership of the UN provided Ireland with the only forum where it could express its concerns across a wide range of international issues including decolonisation, disarmament, human rights and peace keeping. With the emergence of newly independent states in the 1960s, Ireland took up issues of development and equity in economic relations which had assumed increasing importance at the UN.

On three occasions Ireland has served as a non-permanent member of the UN Security Council, in 1962, 1981–1982 and 2001–2002. In January 2003, Ireland had a three year term on the UN Economic and Social Council. Ireland was a member of the UN Commission on Human Rights from 1997–1999 and again from January 2003 for a further three year term.

Former President of Ireland, Mary Robinson, served as UN High Commissioner for Human Rights from 1997 to 2002.

THE INSTITUTIONS OF THE UN

The institutions of the UN are:

- The General Assembly;
- The Security Council;
- The Economic & Social Council;

- The Trusteeship Council;
- The Secretariat; and
- The International Court of Justice.

The General Assembly

The General Assembly is made up of all Member States. It meets once every year. The General Assembly is composed of six main committees dealing with a variety of topics. It is the sixth committee that deals with matters of international law. Resolutions of the General Assembly cannot compel states to take action and are thus of persuasive value only and sometimes referred to as "soft" law.

The Security Council

The Security Council is the body entrusted with primary responsibility for the maintenance of international peace and security. It is composed of five permanent members, viz. China, France, Russia, United Kingdom and United States of America and 10 non-permanent members elected by the General Assembly. Security Council resolutions, unlike resolutions of the General Assembly, are binding on Member States. A nine-member majority is required for a resolution to be carried, with the five permanent members having a veto.

The Economic and Social Council (ECOSOC)

This is the principal organ concerned with economic and social activities carried out by the UN. Not all Member States are represented on this body. It operates a rotating system. This body plays an important role in co-ordinating the activities of what is termed, "the United Nations family of organisations" such as the UN Development Programme, the World Food Programme funds, UNICEF, the World Health Organisation, and UN Educational, Scientific and Cultural Organisation (UNESCO).

The Trusteeship Council

As all trust territories have now attained self-government or independence, the Trusteeship Council suspended operation on November 1, 1994. However, the mechanisms remain in place.

The Secretariat

The Secretariat is the administrative organ of the UN. It is responsible for the day-to-day activities of the UN. It is headed by the Secretary General, who is appointed for a five-year term which may be renewed.

The International Court of Justice (ICJ)

This court which sits in The Hague is also known as the World Court and is the principal judicial organ of the United Nations. In 1946 the ICJ replaced the Permanent Court of International Justice (PCIJ) which had functioned since 1922. The court operates pursuant to a statute annexed to the UN Charter. All Member States of the United Nations are automatically parties to the statute of the ICJ. States may make a declaration under art.36(2) of the statute, accepting as compulsory the jurisdiction of the court in settling legal disputes with other states who have also made a declaration under that article. Many states may make an express reservation from compulsory jurisdiction of the court. A state who has made such a reservation cannot invoke the court's jurisdiction against a state who has accepted the compulsory jurisdiction of the court.

THE WORLD TRADE ORGANISATION

The World Trade Organisation (WTO) which came into being as a result of negotiations in 1995 is the only global international organisation dealing with the rules of trade between nations. It was born out of the General Agreement on Tariffs and Trade (GATT), established in the wake of the Second World War at the Uruguay round of negotiations. GATT is now the principal rule-book of the WTO for trade in goods.

The WTO is a place where member governments go, to try to sort out the trade problems they face with each other.

At its heart are the WTO agreements, negotiated and signed by the bulk of the world's trading nations. These documents provide the legal rules for international commerce.

The system's overriding purpose is to help trade flow as freely as possible without undesirable side-effects.

The system was developed through a series of trade negotiations, or rounds, held under GATT. The first rounds dealt mainly with tariff reductions but later negotiations included other areas such as anti-dumping and non-tariff measures.

The institutions of the WTO

The institutions of the WTO are:

- The Ministerial Conference;
- The General Council;
- Goods Council;
- Services Council;
- The Intellectual Property Council (TRIPS);
- The Secretariat; and
- The Dispute Settlement System.

The Ministerial Conference

This is the topmost decision-making body of the WTO. It usually meets every two years. It brings together all members of the WTO, which are either countries or customs unions. The Ministerial Conference can take decisions on all matters under any of the multilateral trade agreements.

The General Council

This is the WTO's highest level decision-making body. It meets regularly in Geneva to carry out the functions of the WTO. It has representatives (usually ambassadors or equivalent) from all member governments and has the authority to act on behalf of the Ministerial Conference. The General Council also meets, under different rules, as the Dispute Settlement Body and as the Trade Policy Review Body.

Others

At the next level is the Goods Council, the Services Council, and the Intellectual Property Council (TRIPS).

There are numerous specialised committees, working groups and working parties that deal with the individual agreements and other areas such as the environment, development, membership applications and regional trade agreements.

The Secretariat

The Secretariat, which is based in Geneva, is headed by a Director General. The Secretariat does not have the decision-making role that other international bureaucracies are given. The Secretariat's main duties are to supply technical support for the various councils and committees and the Ministerial conferences; to provide technical assistance for developing countries; to analyse world trade; and to explain WTO affairs to the public and media. The Secretariat also provides some forms of legal assistance in the dispute settlement process and advises governments wishing to become members of the WTO.

The Dispute Settlement System

The WTO's procedure for resolving trade disputes under the Dispute Settlement Understanding is vital for enforcing the rules and therefore, for ensuring that trade flows smoothly. Countries bring disputes to the WTO if they think their rights under the agreements are being infringed. Judgments by specially appointed independent experts are based on interpretations of the agreements and individual countries' commitments. The system encourages countries to settle their differences through consultation. Failing settlement, a carefully mapped out, stage-by-stage procedure that includes the possibility of a ruling by a panel of experts, and the chance to appeal the ruling on points of law, can be utilised.

The Courts

6

This Chapter outlines the structure, composition and jurisdiction of the courts in the Irish legal system. Reference is also made to the Dáil Courts and the courts of Saorstát Éireann which are now of historic interest only.

The History of the Courts

The Dáil Courts

The Dáil Éireann Courts (Winding Up) Act 1923 defines the Dáil Courts as meaning any court that was constituted under a decree made in the year 1920 by the Minister for Home Affairs.

The establishment of the Dáil Courts arose from the widespread insurrection and insurgency that prevailed against British rule in Ireland from 1919 to 1921 and which made it virtually impossible to operate the court system either in Dublin or the provinces. Matters were further complicated by the fact that the parliamentary assembly of the Irish nationalists, Dáil Éireann, had passed decrees in 1920 establishing their own courts, the courts of Dáil Éireann or the Dáil Courts.

These Dáil Courts which comprised Parish Courts, District Courts, a Circuit Court and a Supreme Court had no validity from the point of view of the governing law and were suppressed by the British authorities as far as possible.

In June 1922, the British formally handed over the control of the court system. The Dáil Court system could now have been operated freely but in July and October 1922 the Cabinet decided to abolish the Dáil Éireann Courts and they were wound up in 1923.

The courts of Saorstát Éireann

The courts system that was to be established under Saorstát Éireann, in the 1922 Constitution, is similar in structure to the current court system.

Article 64 of the Constitution of Saorstát Éireann provided that the judicial power of the Irish Free State was to be exercised and justice was to be administered in the public courts established by the Oireachtas. The Courts of Justice Act 1924 established these courts in accordance with Art.64 which provided for both courts of first instance and courts of appeal (see Pts I, II and III of the 1924 Act). These were a District Court, a Circuit Court, a High Court, a Court of Criminal Appeal and a Supreme Court.

THE CURRENT COURTS SYSTEM

The courts and their structure

Article 34 of the Constitution provides that justice is to be administered in courts established by law and save in special and limited cases as may be prescribed by law, shall be administered in public. When a case is not heard in public it is said to be heard "in camera".

The current system of courts is set out in Arts 34 and 38 of Bunreacht na hÉireann, the 1937 Constitution. The structure of the courts in the Irish legal system is hierarchical, comprising superior courts and inferior or lower courts.

The superior courts are:

- The Supreme Court; and
- The High Court.

The lower or inferior courts are:

- The Circuit Court; and
- The District Court.

These courts are collectively referred to as the *ordinary courts* as distinct from the *special courts* envisaged by Art.38. See Art.38.3.1° which provides:

> *Special courts* may be established by law for the trial of offences in cases where it may be determined in accordance with such law that the *ordinary courts* are inadequate to secure the effective administration of justice and the preservation of peace and order. (Emphasis added).

The Special Criminal Court was established under this provision.

Whereas all the courts in the legal system were envisaged by the Constitution, the superior courts were specifically provided for. Thus, no enacting legislation was required to formally establish them. (See Arts 34.2, 34.3.1° and 34.4.1°). However, although the Constitution allowed for the creation of the District Court and the Circuit Court (see Art.34.3.4°) the Courts (Establishment and Constitution) Act 1961 formally established them. The Constitution merely referred to them as courts of *local and limited jurisdiction*—local referring to the locality in which they would have jurisdiction and limiting their jurisdiction to hear only certain matters and limiting the awards they can grant and the penalties/sentences they can impose.

Similarly, although Art.38.3.1° allowed for the creation of the Special Criminal Court, enacting legislation was required to formally establish it. See the Offences Against the State Act 1939.

The jurisdiction of the courts

The jurisdiction of the courts must be considered from a number of different aspects. Jurisdiction of a court may be civil or criminal, it may be an original (first instance) or an appellate jurisdiction. Jurisdiction will be limited to the type of matters a particular court hears, the level of awards it may grant, the type of penalties it may impose, and in the case of the District Court and the Circuit Court jurisdiction, will be determined on a locality basis. The following table should help students to get a grasp of the various aspects of jurisdiction:

Civil jurisdiction—(can hear civil matters)	All courts
Criminal jurisdiction—(can hear criminal matters)	All courts
First instance jurisdiction—(the court the matter comes to first)	All courts have a first instance jurisdiction in some matters
Appellate jurisdiction—(may hear appeals from lower courts)	All courts except the District Court
Local and limited jurisdiction (Local—limited to certain geographical areas: Limited—limited to certain matters.	Applies to the District Court and to the Circuit Court only.

THE DISTRICT COURT

At the bottom of the hierarchy or pyramid is the District Court which has the largest number of courts. There is a District Court in nearly every town of any size in the country.

It sits with a presiding judge but without a jury. The District Court has a President and 52 District judges.

Although this court is the lowest court in the system it handles an enormous case-load.

For operational purposes the country is divided into the Dublin Metropolitan District and 23 District Court Districts. Each District is sub-divided into District areas and a court must be held in each area. For example, County Wexford has four District areas, namely District area of Wexford (town), District area of New Ross, District area of Enniscorthy and District area of Gorey.

The President of the District Court organises the affairs of the court and is an *ex officio* judge of the Circuit Court. Whether it is hearing civil or criminal matters this court is referred to as the District Court.

Jurisdiction

The District Court has a civil and a criminal jurisdiction. An appeal from the District Court lies to the Circuit Court. The District Court also has jurisdiction to state a case to the High Court.

Criminal jurisdiction

In criminal matters the District Court is limited to hearing summary or minor offences. Offences are classed as summary (minor) or indictable (non-minor). There is a further type of offence which is hybrid in nature. The District Court has jurisdiction to hear these hybrid offences *provided* three conditions are satisfied: the DPP must consent to the summary trial; the District Judge has to form an opinion that the facts proved or alleged constitute a minor offence fit to be tried summarily; and the accused must consent to summary trial (s.2 of the Criminal Justice Act 1952).

The District Court's jurisdiction in criminal matters is also *locally* limited, which means a particular District Court (in a District Court Area) may only hear offence if one of the following criteria is satisfied:

(1) The accused resides in the District Court Area.
(2) The accused was arrested in the District Court Area.
(3) The offence was committed in the District Court Area.

See *O'Brien v O'Halloran* (unreported, High Court, November 16, 1999).

Civil jurisdiction

In civil matters the District Court is *limited* to awarding compensation up to a maximum of €6,348.69 (however, the monetary jurisdiction of the District Court can be increased if both parties so agree in writing).

The District Court is also *limited* in the types of civil cases that it can hear. It has jurisdiction to hear cases involving contract disputes and claims in tort, provided the amount claimed is less than €6,348.69. It cannot, however, hear certain types of tort cases such as defamation. Neither has it the jurisdiction to grant decrees of judicial separation or divorce. It has jurisdiction to deal with some family law matters such as guardianship, access, custody and maintenance orders, and make grant orders such as barring, protection and safety orders under the Domestic Violence Act 1996, care orders regarding children under the Child Care Act 1991 (as amended), and hear certain types of landlord and tenant cases such as actions for ejectment for non-payment of rent provided the rent is below a certain level per annum. The District Court has jurisdiction to deal with the renewal of liquor licences.

The Circuit Court

The Circuit Court is the next court in the pyramid. There are eight Circuits in the country. These are the Dublin Circuit, the Cork Circuit, the Eastern Circuit, the Midland Circuit, the South-Eastern Circuit, the Western Circuit, the South-Western Circuit and the Northern Circuit.

The Circuit Court sits in various towns in the Circuit with the judges assigned to each Circuit travelling to the different towns in that Circuit a number of times each year. In Dublin and Cork there is a permanent Circuit Court sitting.

The Circuit Court has a President who is also an *ex officio* judge of the High Court.

This court sits with a judge in civil cases and with a judge and a jury in criminal cases. When it is exercising its appellate jurisdiction (hearing appeals from the District Court), it sits with a judge only and no jury.

It is generally referred to as the Circuit Court whether hearing civil or criminal matters. However, there is a designated Circuit Criminal Court in Dublin. There is also a designated Circuit Family Law Court sitting in Phoenix House, Smithfield, Dublin 7.

Jurisdiction

Like the District Court, the Circuit Court is a court of local and limited jurisdiction. The Circuit Court has a civil and a criminal jurisdiction. It has an original (first instance) and an appellate jurisdiction. An appeal from the Circuit Court lies to the High Court. The Circuit Court has jurisdiction to state a case to the Supreme Court.

Criminal jurisdiction

The Circuit Court's jurisdiction in criminal matters is to try indictable offences and minor offences on appeal from the District Court. However, because it is a court of *limited* jurisdiction it cannot hear all indictable matters. There are some exceptions that are reserved exclusively to the jurisdiction of the High Court. These reserved offences are treason, murder, attempted murder, conspiracy to murder, rape and aggravated sexual assault.

Where an offence is being tried in the Circuit Court there will be a judge and jury (Art.38.5 of the Constitution).

Civil jurisdiction

The Circuit Court has jurisdiction to make awards not exceeding €38,092.14. The limit of jurisdiction can be increased by consent of the parties or the excess of jurisdiction may be abandoned by the party bringing the action (the plaintiff). When hearing disputes involving gender discrimination the Circuit Court has unlimited jurisdiction in the level of award it can make.

The Circuit Court can hear all types of claims in contract and tort, including the tort of defamation. The Circuit Court may hear disputes regarding land provided the rateable valuation of the land is less than €254. When dealing with family law matters, the Circuit Court is referred to as the Circuit Family Court. The Circuit Court has concurrent jurisdiction with the High Court to grant decrees of nullity, judicial separation and divorce. The Circuit Court is also given exclusive jurisdiction in certain landlord and tenant matters.

The Circuit Court has an equitable jurisdiction; this means it may grant injunctions and decrees of specific performance.

The Circuit Court has jurisdiction regarding applications for new liquor licences.

The Circuit Court hears appeals from the Employment Appeals Tribunal (EAT) and the Equality Tribunal.

Appellate jurisdiction

There are two types of appeal that a party to an action in the District Court may bring to the Circuit Court whether the subject matter is civil or criminal:

- *De novo* hearing.
- Appeal on a point of law.

A *de novo* hearing is a full rehearing on matters of both fact and law. All the witnesses are heard and any evidence given orally in the lower court is again heard. The parties in a hearing *de novo* thus get a second opportunity to have their case tried.

An appeal on a point of law requires a higher court to determine an issue of law rather than fact. In this type of appeal the findings of fact by the lower court should not be disturbed. This type of appeal is saying the trial judge may have made a mistake in law. The witnesses do not attend, there is no oral evidence; rather the trial proceeds on the basis of transcripts of the evidence given in the lower court.

Where the Circuit Court, at the conclusion of a trial, states a case to the Supreme Court this may have the same effect as an appeal. This type of case stated is referred to as "an appeal by way of case stated" as opposed to a "consultative case stated" which occurs during the trial but before the conclusion.

The appeal of a decision of the District Court to the Circuit Court does not change the nature of the case. It still remains a District Court level case and any awards or penalties will be those within the jurisdictional levels of the District Court.

The decision of the Circuit Court, on appeal, is final and conclusive and cannot be further appealed to the High Court other than on a point of law.

The High Court

Above the Circuit Court is the High Court. There is one High Court exercising jurisdiction over the whole country. The High Court generally sits in the Four Courts in Dublin but visits other centres such as Cork and Galway and sometimes goes on Circuit, usually when hearing appeals from the Circuit Court.

When hearing criminal cases the High Court is known as the Central Criminal Court. When exercising its appellate jurisdiction in criminal matter the High Court is known as the Court of Criminal Appeal.

The High Court generally sits with one judge in civil matters and with a judge and jury in criminal matters but may sit with three judges in some cases.

The High Court has a President who organises the affairs of the court and who is an *ex officio* judge of the Supreme Court.

Jurisdiction

The High Court has jurisdiction to hear civil and criminal matters. It has a first instance jurisdiction and an appellate jurisdiction. An appeal from the High Court lies to the Supreme Court and the High Court may state a case to the Supreme Court.

Criminal jurisdiction

In criminal matters the High Court has jurisdiction in respect of reserved offences; these reserved offences are treason, murder, attempted murder, conspiracy to murder, rape and aggravated sexual assault.

Civil jurisdiction

The High Court has jurisdiction to hear civil matters where the claim is in excess of €38,000. As previously mentioned, the High Court has concurrent jurisdiction with the Circuit Court to grant decrees of judicial separation, divorce and nullity. The High Court has jurisdiction in wardship applications and applications under the Companies Acts. This jurisdiction is given to the High Court expressly by The Courts (Supplemental Provisions) Act 1961 (s.9(1)). Habeus corpus applications are made to the High Court.

Constitutional challenges to the validity of legislation are within the jurisdiction of the High Court. This is expressly provided for by Art.34.3.2° of the Constitution.

The High Court has a supervisory role over decisions made by the lower courts such as the Circuit Court and the District Court. The High Court has a similar supervisory role over decisions made by administrative bodies such as local authorities. This supervisory role is referred to as judicial review. Legislation may also be judicially reviewed by the High Court.

First instance or original jurisdiction

Article 34.3.1° provides that the High Court shall be invested with "full original jurisdiction in and power to determine all matters and questions whether of law or fact, civil or criminal". However, the meaning of *all* has to be interpreted as meaning all matters that are justiciable. Justiciable means capable of being tried by a court or able to be settled by applying principles of law. (See Supreme Court in *Tormey v Ireland* [1985] I.R. 289; [1985] I.L.R.M. 375).

Full original jurisdiction means that any case in theory could choose to come to the High Court at first instance. If all matters that were justiciable were to come at first instance to the High Court it would be impractical. The case of *Ward v Kinahan Electrical Ltd* [1984] I.R. 292 makes it clear that Art.34.3.1° should not be given an interpretation that would require the High Court to hear all justiciable matters.

Appellate jurisdiction

The High Court has jurisdiction to hear appeals from the Circuit Court and appeals by way of case stated from the District Court (see ss.37 and 38 of the Courts of Justice Act 1936 regarding appeals from the Circuit Court).

Both ss.37 and 38 provide for a rehearing. However, s.37 provides that evidence that was not given and received at the Circuit Court hearing cannot be given or received at the hearing of the appeal except with the special leave of the judge hearing the appeal. The decision of the High Court on appeal from the Circuit Court is final and conclusive and not appealable (see s.39). In other words if a decision of the Circuit Court is appealed to the High Court it cannot be further appealed to the Supreme Court.

The High Court has jurisdiction to hear a case stated from the District Court which, as already started, can have the same effect as an appeal.

THE SUPREME COURT

At the apex of the pyramid is the Supreme Court. The Supreme Court is established under the Constitution (see Art.34). The Supreme Court may be a five-judge court or a three-judge court and is, therefore, a collegiate court. The Supreme Court does not sit with a jury. In constitutional cases the Supreme Court sits with five judges. Each judge delivers a judgment and the decision of the court is that of the majority.

Instead of a President this court has a Chief Justice who organises the affairs of the court. As stated above, the President of the High Court is an *ex officio* judge of this court and other High Court judges by invitation may sit on this court but not in constitutional cases.

Jurisdiction

The Supreme Court is primarily an appellate court and therefore, its original jurisdiction is very limited. In order to appeal a decision to the Supreme Court, the leave of the High Court must be obtained. The Supreme Court has jurisdiction to hear case stated applications from the Circuit Court and from the High Court.

Decisions of the Supreme Court according to Art.34.4.6° are final and conclusive. However, Art.34.4.6° must be read in the light of Art.243 of the EC Treaty (ex Art.177 of the Treaty of Rome) which provides for a referral from a national court of a Member State to the European of Court of Justice. See *Re Greendale Developments Ltd (No.3)* [2000] 2 I.R. 514 where the question of the finality and conclusiveness of a decision of the Supreme Court having regard to Art.243 was considered. Article 34.4.6° must also be read in light of Ireland's commitment under the European Convention on Human Rights.

Original jurisdiction

An important part of the Supreme Court's original jurisdiction concerns reference of Bills under Art.26 of the Constitution. A decision by the Supreme Court to the effect that a Bill is constitutional renders it immune from future constitutional challenge.

Pursuant to Art.12.3.1° the incapacity of the President to continue in office has to be established to the satisfaction of the Supreme Court.

Although Art.34.4.1° refers to the Supreme Court in terms of it being the court of final appeal, nonetheless, it was made clear in *State (Browne) v Feran* [1967] I.R. 147 this was not to be taken to mean that the Supreme Court is only a court of appeal. This case held that the Supreme Court does have limited original jurisdiction. That this is so is clear from Arts 12.3.1° and 26.2.1° of the Constitution.

Article 36 of the Constitution provides that the "distribution of jurisdiction and business" among the Supreme Court, the High Court and the judges shall be regulated in accordance with law. There is a difference of opinion as to whether Art.36 of the Constitution allows jurisdiction other than set out above to be added to the jurisdiction of the Supreme Court. Two cases that give opposing views are *State (Browne) v Feran* [1976] I.R. 147 where it was stated that Art.36 would so allow, and *Dunnes Stores Ireland Co v Ryan* (unreported, Supreme Court, February 8, 2000) where it was stated that it was not open to the Supreme Court to determine an issue of constitutional law other than by way of appeal from the High Court.

Appellate jurisdiction

The appellate jurisdiction of the Supreme Court is set out in Art.34.4.3°. The Supreme Court shall, subject to exceptions proscribed by law, have appellate jurisdiction from all decisions of the High Court. However, this article must be read in conjunction with Art.34.4.4° which states that no law shall be enacted, excepting from the appellate jurisdiction of the Supreme Court, matters which involve questions on the constitutionality of any law.

The Courts of Justice Act 1936 (s.39—as re-enacted by s.48 of the Courts (Supplemental Provisions) Act 1961) is an example of an exception proscribed by law. This provision states that an appeal from the Circuit Court to the High Court shall be final and conclusive and not appealable and thus, it cannot be appealed to the Supreme Court. In *Eamonn Andrews Production Ltd v Gaiety Theatre Enterprises Ltd* [1973] I.R. 295, this exception to the appellate jurisdiction of the Supreme Court was held to be a valid exception.

A further exception to the appellate jurisdiction of the Supreme Court was identified in *Campus Oil Ltd v Minister for Industry and Energy* [1983] I.R. 82 where it was held that questions on the interpretation of an EC Treaty should be referred to the European Court of Justice and not to the Supreme Court.

Any enactment that seeks to create an exception to the appellate jurisdiction of the Supreme Court must be clear and unambiguous. See *People (Attorney General) v Conmey* [1975] I.R. 341.

The Court of Criminal Appeal

The Court of Criminal Appeal has, as its name indicates, a criminal appellate jurisdiction only. This court is a creature of statute being created by the Courts (Establishment and Constitution) Act 1961 (s.3). The Court of Criminal Appeal hears appeals from the Circuit Court, the Central Criminal Court and the Special Criminal Court.

Any person found guilty by one of those courts does not have an automatic right of appeal, and in order to appeal, a certificate of appeal must be obtained from the trial judge, or if the trial judge refuses to give this certificate the leave of the Court of Criminal Appeal must be obtained.

The Court of Criminal Appeal sits with one Supreme Court judge and two High Court judges. The decision of the court is by majority and only one judgment is given. This court sometimes hears appeals from court martial and when it does it is known as the Courts Martial Appeals Court.

The hearing of the appeals is by transcript of the evidence. Only one judgment is delivered and it is by the senior judge. The decision of that court is final unless the court is prepared to grant a certificate for an appeal to the Supreme Court. Such a certificate is only granted if the court is satisfied to certify that the case involved a question or point of law of exceptional public importance and that it is desirable in the public interest that an appeal should be taken to the Supreme Court.

The Special Criminal Court

The Special Criminal Court does not so much have a place in the pyramid as such but rather is the court that deals with criminal matters where *ordinary courts* are inadequate to secure the effective administration of justice and the preservation of peace and order.

The Special Criminal Court has 11 members consisting of four High Court judges, three Circuit Court judges and four District Court judges. This court sits with three judges and does not have a jury. This court delivers one judgment.

The legal basis for this court is Art.38.3.1° but legislation was necessary to formally establish it. This was done in the form of s.35 of the Offences against the State Act 1939 which confers on government the power to issue a proclamation. The issuing of this proclamation brings Pt V of the Act into force. Part V allows for the establishment of special criminal courts and once in force it will remain in force until annulled by resolution of the Dáil Éireann. The proclamation under which the current Special Criminal Court exists was issued in 1972.

The Special Criminal Court deals with what are known as "scheduled offences". Scheduled offences generally involve subversive crime. The current list of scheduled offences includes any offence under the Criminal Damage Act 1991; an offence under Pt 7 of the Criminal Justice Act 2006 (excluding conspiracy); any offence under the Explosive Substances Act 1883; any offence under the Firearms Acts 1925 to 2006; and any offence under the Offences Against the State Act 1939.

If the offence charged is not a scheduled offence, the DPP may certify that in his opinion, the ordinary courts are inadequate to secure the administration of justice and the preservation of public peace and order. Once such a certificate is issued, the case must be transferred from the ordinary courts to the Special Criminal Court.

An appeal against conviction or sentence by a Special Criminal Court may, with leave, be taken to the Court of Criminal Appeal.

The Children's Court

The Children's or Juvenile Court is the court that children or minors appear before when charged with criminal offences. Crime is generally considered an adult business, nonetheless, the law recognises the liability of certain minors for criminal offences.

The court system in Ireland does not have a dedicated juvenile court. Instead the District Court doubles up as a Children's Court or Juvenile Court for both summary and indictable offences. Part 7 of the Children's Act 2001 provides that when hearing charges against children the District Court is to be known as the Children's Court and is to sit in a different building or room in which other court cases are being heard on the day (s.71). Children's cases are held "in camera".

The Criminal Court of Justice Complex

The establishment of the new Criminal Court complex in Dublin 7, the Criminal Court of Justice, which was opened in January 2010 concentrates the administration of criminal justice, both national and local, into one dedicated facility. The Central Criminal Court, Court of Criminal Appeal, Special Criminal Court, Dublin Circuit Criminal Court and Dublin District Criminal Court will all be located in this facility.

This court is merely a complex or building to house the various courts hearing criminal matters and does not affect their jurisdiction.

CASE STATED

A case stated is an application whereby a judge of a lower court poses a question or questions of law to a higher court once removed. Thus, a case stated from the District Court will lie to the High Court and a case stated from the Circuit Court lies to the Supreme Court. A case stated from the High Court for obvious reason lies to the Supreme Court.

Case stated applications are restricted to matters of law. Findings of fact by the trial judge are conclusive. Occasionally, however, the point of law will be concerned with the fact because some questions are mixed questions of law and fact.

There are two types of case stated:

1. A consultative case stated.
2. An appeal by way of case stated.

A consultative case stated arises *before* a determination is made by the trial judge, that is before a trial judge reaches a decision in the case. The jurisdiction for a consultative case stated is found in s.52 of the Courts Supplemental Provisions Act 1961.

An appeal by way of case stated arises *after* a decision is made in a case and where it is felt the trial judge made an error of law. The jurisdiction for an appeal by way of case stated is found in s.2 of the Summary Jurisdiction Act 1857, as amended by s.51 of the Courts Supplemental Provisions Act 1961. Such an appeal can be taken against a conviction or an acquittal.

The application to state a case has procedural requirements that must be strictly adhered to otherwise the higher court will not have jurisdiction to hear the application.

The application to state a case is made to the trial judge and the trial judge can only refuse the application if it is considered to be frivolous or vexatious. If the judge does refuse to state a case the applicant can ask the judge to issue a certificate of refusal and this must be issued if it is requested. This certificate enables the applicant to go to the High Court seeking an order requiring the trial judge and the respondent to show cause why a case should not be stated. See, for example, *State (Turley) v O'Floinn* [1968] I.R. 245.

Practice and Procedure in the Courts

Introduction

Practice and procedure for the various courts is set down either in statute and/or in the Rules of Court, enacted pursuant to statutory instruments and will vary depending on whether the court is exercising a civil or a criminal jurisdiction.

The Rules are drawn up by a Rules Committee. The Rules Committee was first established by the Judicature (Ireland) Act 1877 and at that time applied to the superior courts only. Statutes such as the Court of Justice Acts 1927 and 1936 established a Rules Committee for the other courts. These Rules Committees have statutory powers, with the concurrence of the Minister for Justice, Equality and Law Reform to review, amend and make rules for their own court.

Each court has its own set of Rules. Thus you have the District Court Rules, the Circuit Court Rules and the Rules of the Superior Courts which applies to the High Court and the Supreme Court.

These Rules set out how actions are to be commenced, what the originating documents are, the pre-trial procedure, the interlocutory procedures, conduct of the trial itself and the appellate procedure.

Commencement of Proceedings

So how do cases get into court? Simply put, it takes paperwork to get matters into court, be it civil or criminal actions. This paperwork is referred to as the originating document.

There is also a time-frame within which actions must be commenced. The general rule for the commencement of criminal actions is that prosecutions for minor or summary offences must be commenced within six months from the commission of the offence. There are some statutory exceptions to this whereby the limitation period is extended to one year or two years. In the case of non-minor or indictable offences there is no limitation period for the commencement of prosecution.

Commencement of civil actions is governed by the Statute of Limitations Act 1957, the Statute of Limitations (Amendment) Act 1991 and the Statute of Limitations (Amendment) Act 2000. See also the Civil Liability and Courts Act 2004 which reduced the limitation period for personal injury actions to two years. The limitation periods within which an action may be commenced are as follows:

Personal injury actions .... 2 years

Actions in tort .... 6 years

Actions for breach of contract .... 6 years

Actions for recovery of land .... 12 years

Time starts running for the purpose of the statute from the date on which the cause of action accrued or from the date of knowledge. In the case of young persons time does not start running until they have achieved their 18th birthday.

PRACTICE AND PROCEDURE IN CIVIL MATTERS

In civil actions the paperwork is called the *pleadings*. A pleading is a written statement of the material facts which each party will rely on to make his/her claim or to make his/her defence. Pleadings also serve a tactical purpose. The whole purpose of a pleading is to save time and cost in the court so that the parties and the trial judge will know what the issues are and to ensure that a case is won on its merits and not because one of the parties has been taken by surprise which is sometimes referred to as "trial by ambush".

If a case is pleaded properly it may result in the defendant making an offer to settle the action. Many cases are resolved by settlement and it is only a percentage of cases that actually go to trial.

District Court pleadings

In the District Court the originating document is called a *civil summons*. The other documents that form the District Court pleadings are:

- The indorsement of claim; and
- Notice of intention to defend.

The indorsement of claim
This is a pre-printed form in which the details such as name and address of the plaintiff, what the claim is about and what remedy or relief sought is set out.

Notice of intention to defend
If the defendant intends to defend or dispute the claim he/she serves a notice of intention to defend on the plaintiff.

This is usually the end of the paperwork in the District Court. However, there is provision in the District Court Rules for the service of a notice for particulars, an order for discovery and a third party notice.

The summons must be issued and served. It is taken to the appropriate District Court office, where a fee is paid, the document is stamped, given a number and entered in the District Court book. The original is then served on the defendant or on his solicitor either personally or by registered post/prepaid post and an affidavit of service must be prepared.

Circuit Court pleadings

In the Circuit Court the originating summons is called a Civil Bill. There are different types of Civil Bill. The Rules of the Circuit Court identifies 13 types which should be used in a particular case. Most actions are commenced by what is known as an Ordinary Civil Bill. Where a claim for equitable relief is pursued an Equitable Civil Bill is used. These are the two most common types of Civil Bill used.

Indorsement of claim
The Civil Bill is accompanied by an indorsement of claim which sets out a full statement of the plaintiff's claim against the defendant in numbered paragraphs.

Notice of appearance
Following service of a summons, the defendant has to file a notice of appearance. The notice of appearance a simple one page pro forma document.

Defence
If the defendant has a defence to the claim of the plaintiff it is set out in numbered paragraphs in the defence. Essentially the defendant denies the claim of the plaintiff and pleads his/her defence.

Counterclaim
When a plaintiff issues proceedings against a defendant and that defendant has a cause of action against the plaintiff deriving from the same set of facts, it is open to the defendant to raise this by way of counterclaim in the existing action. A counterclaim is in effect a separate action, but the Judicature

(Ireland) Act 1877 allows the defendant to raise it in the plaintiff's action in order to simplify court proceedings.

The other documents that may form part of the pleadings in the Circuit Court are a third party notice, third party defence, notice for further and better particulars, reply to particulars, discovery or interrogatories.

The Civil Bill must be issued and served. It is taken to the appropriate Circuit Court office, a fee is paid, the Bill is stamped, numbered, recorded and served and an affidavit of service prepared. The Civil Bill must be served within a year. If it is not served within the year it must be renewed. Time does not stop for the purposes of the Statute of Limitations 1957 until the Bill is served.

High Court pleadings

In the High Court the originating document may either be a summons, a petition or a motion. There are three different types of originating summons that may be used depending on the subject matter of the case. The Rules of the Superior Court 1986 gives guidance on this matter.

These three types of summons are a plenary summons, a special summons or a summary summons (the latter not to be confused with a summary offence or summary trial in criminal matters).

Personal injuries summons

In addition to the above originating documents, since 2004 there is a further originating document entitled a personal injuries summons (see the Civil Liability and Courts Act 2004). Proceedings in the District Court, Circuit Court and the High Court in respect of a personal injury action must now be commenced by way of a personal injuries summons. As noted in the section on the Injuries Board (see at p.144) proceedings may only be brought to the courts on foot of an authorisation by the Injuries Board.

Motion

Proceedings in appropriate cases may also be commenced by originating motion. The documents required are a notice of motion and grounding affidavit. Proceedings commenced by way of the motion procedure tend to be disposed of in a shorter period of time.

Petition

Petitions are used where there is no identifiable defendant or where proceedings need to be brought to the notice of a large number of people. It is used regularly in company law proceedings and in other matters that need to be brought to the notice of the general public. Whereas there is no standard form for a petition, certain indorsements are necessary regarding address and occupation or description of the petitioner.

The other paperwork is a general indorsement of claim, a statement of claim, an appearance, a defence, notice for further and better particulars and reply to notice for particulars, third party notice, discovery, interrogatories and affidavits (where appropriate).

In the High Court documents are issued by being brought to the Central Office of the High Court in Dublin. They are stamped there and they must be served by the solicitor instructed by the plaintiff on the defendant and an affidavit of service prepared. With High Court proceedings, time stops for the purposes of the Statute of Limitations when the summons is issued.

Notice of appearance

As noted for the Circuit Court.

General indorsement of claim

The general indorsement of claim sets out in summary form only the nature of the claim (it is usually three to four lines stating, for example, damages for personal injury or damages or breach of contract and the nature of the relief sought).

Statement of claim

The statement of claim is similar to the indorsement of claim in the Circuit Court. It is document where the plaintiff's case is pleaded.

Defence

As noted for the Circuit Court.

Notice for particulars

A notice for particulars may issue from the plaintiff to the defendant or vice versa. Particulars are generally sought by a defendant in respect of a plaintiff's statement of claim (indorsement of claim for a Circuit Court matter) or defence. The purpose of particulars is to define the issues between the parties, to confine the evidence of the trial to the matters relevant to those issues and to ensure that neither party is taken at a disadvantage by the introduction of matters not fairly to be ascertained from the pleadings. The particulars sought must relate to matters pleaded or matters said to be within the four corners of the pleadings. Particulars will request such information as, for example, where the plaintiff works, what are his/her earnings, is he/she in receipt of social welfare payments, what is his/her RSI number, what hospital was the plaintiff treated in, what doctors/consultants were involved. The parties are entitled to know the range of evidence but not the actual evidence.

Replies to particulars

Replies to particulars are simply the replies to the particulars requested. Where a party requested to reply to particulars fails to reply or fails to reply in sufficient detail, the party requesting the particulars may seek an order of the court compelling replies. Failure to comply with such an order of the court may result in a staying of the plaintiff's case or the striking out of the defendant's defence.

Discovery

Discovery is a process whereby parties are able to obtain from each other a list of documents necessary to the proceedings that are in the custody or control (possession, power or procurement) of the parties. Under the Rules voluntary discovery must first be sought and if the party so requested fails, refuses or neglects to provide discovery the party seeking discovery may apply to the court for an order compelling discovery. Failure to comply with such order of court may result in a staying of the plaintiff's case or the striking out of the defendant's defence.

Interrogatories

Interrogatories are a method of discovering material facts. Written questions are delivered by one party to the other party relating to a matter in issue between the parties. Interrogatories must be phrased in such a way that the question asked it is capable of only two answers—"yes" or "no". Interrogatories look for the answer to a very narrow specific fact.

Affidavit

An affidavit is a sworn court document whereby a party to legal proceedings sets out in a particular format certain information. Documents in support also form part of an affidavit as exhibits annexed to the affidavit.

PRACTICE AND PROCEDURE IN CRIMINAL MATTERS

The first thing to be noted is that all criminal offences at first instance appear before a judge of the District Court. In appropriate cases the matter is then sent forward to either the Circuit Criminal Court or the Central Criminal Court.

Prosecutions, with some exceptions, are brought by the Director of Public Prosecutions or by a member of An Garda Síochána in the name of the DPP.

As previously mentioned, minor offences are tried in the District Court whereas indictable (more serious) offences will be tried in the Circuit Criminal Court or the Central Criminal Court.

Commencement of criminal prosecution

There are three different types of originating document in order to commence criminal prosecutions. These are a summons, a warrant and a charge sheet. None of these are superior to the other they are merely different processes to be used as is appropriate and whose sole purpose is the securing of the presence of the accused before the court. Because this is the sole purpose of the summons, warrant or charge sheet technical defects are irrelevant where the accused appears as appearance is said to cure defects. See *DPP v Clein* [1983] I.L.R.M. 76.

In order to have one of these documents issued it is necessary for the DPP, the prosecuting Garda or other prosecutor to lay an information (make a complaint) or an application to the appropriate person. The appropriate person will be a judge or a District Court clerk.

The summons

There are two types of summons. A summons pursuant to the Petty Sessions (Ireland) Act 1851 (the "1851 Act") and a summons pursuant to the Courts (No.3) Act 1986 (the "1986 Act") (the latter is referred to as the "Administrative" Procedure). These are two very different procedures. If you utilise the 1851 Act, the complaint is made on oath to a District Judge. Under the 1986 Act, the complaint (which is called an "application") is made to a District Court Clerk in the area that has jurisdiction in the matter or to the Central Administration Processing Unit. The Central Administration Processing Unit is an office of the Courts Service designated for the purposes of receiving applications and issuing summons pursuant to s.49 of the Civil Liability and Courts Act 2004.

An information (complaint) or application alleging a criminal offence is simply a statement of facts constituting an offence. The statement sets out the particulars, such as the name and address of the person alleged to have committed the offence, the basic facts of the offence alleged, and the date and place of the commission of the offence.

In the case of a minor offence there is generally a six-month time limit from the date of the commission of the alleged offence to the laying of the information or the making of the application (s.10(4) of 1851 Act). If the complaint is made outside this six-month period it is a complete defence to the charge. (See *The Minister for Agriculture v Norgro Ltd* [1980] I.R. 55. In the case of an offence which may, at the election of the prosecution, be tried either summarily or on indictment, this six-month time limit does not apply (s.177 of the Criminal Procedure Act 2006).

If the summons procedure is utilised the summons must be served on the defendant. The summons, once obtained, has a shelf life of 12 months, after which it expires and must be renewed.

The charge sheet

The charge sheet procedure is regulated by Ord.17 of the District Court Rules. In *Attorney General (McDonnell) v Higgins* [1964] I.R. 374, it was stated that it is only when the charge sheet is put before the District judge that it becomes a document of the court. See also, *State (Lynch) v Ballagh* [1986] I.R. 203.

The charge sheet may be used in the following three situations:

(1) Where an accused has been arrested without warrant.
(2) Where an accused has been arrested on foot of a warrant charging an offence.
(3) Where the accused is already in remand in respect of other alleged offences and the Gardaí wish to bring an additional charge against him.

Particulars of the offence alleged must be set out on the charge sheet and the accused must be brought before a judge having jurisdiction to deal with the matter as soon as practicable.

The use of the charge sheet procedure does not dispense with the need for a complaint to be made. That this is so was made clear in *Attorney General (McDonnell) v Higgins* [1964] I.R. 374. Thus, the complaint must be made to the judge before whom the accused is brought.

The warrant

The warrant procedure is the more appropriate procedure to be utilised where the offence alleged is more serious. An arrest warrant is issued and the accused is brought on foot of it before the court as soon as possible, whereas the summons merely directs the accused to appear. Prior to the issue of the arrest warrant, an information is sworn on oath and in writing to a judge of the District Court who issues the arrest warrant. The accused is then arrested on foot of the warrant and brought before the District Court as soon as practicable and sent forward from that court to either the Circuit Criminal Court or the Central Criminal Court.

ACCESS TO THE COURTS

Access to the courts is a constitutional right of every citizen. However, without financial assistance some citizens would be denied access to the courts. The provision of legal aid services was thus introduced. Legal aid in criminal matters was introduced by the Criminal Justice (Legal Aid) Act 1962 and was extended by the Criminal (Procedure) Amendment Act 1973. Legal aid in civil matters was introduced by the Civil Legal Aid Act 1995 following the case of *Airey v Ireland* (1979) 2 E.H.R.R. 30.

LEGAL AID

Civil legal aid

The Legal Aid Board provides legal services in relation to civil law matters to eligible persons. Legal aid is available in relation to most civil matters, but there are some exceptions. Legal advice is also provided. To qualify for legal aid services, a person must satisfy the Board's financial eligibility requirements. They must also satisfy the Board that their case has merit.

Legal advice may also be available in relation to most civil matters. It consists of any oral or written advice given by a solicitor or a barrister in civil matters. It can include writing letters and acting in negotiations with other persons. The advice is provided by solicitors in the Board's law centre network.

Legal aid means representation by a solicitor or barrister in civil proceedings in the various courts. It is also available for representation before the Refugee Appeals Tribunal. However, it is not granted automatically. If a party requires representation for a court case, the Board will consider if it is reasonable to grant legal aid. A merits test applies. This test is applied to each individual case. If the Board considers that it is reasonable to grant legal aid, a legal aid certificate will be issued which provides for legal representation. Legal aid is provided by solicitors employed by the Board in its law centres. In certain family law and asylum cases, legal aid may be provided by solicitors in private practice who are contracted by the Board and placed on a panel for this purpose. Barristers are chosen from a panel maintained by the Legal Aid Board.

In order to qualify financially for legal services from the Board, a party, as already noted, must satisfy a means test, and their annual disposable income must currently be less than €18,000. In order to calculate disposable income, the Board will take into account gross income (whether in the form of wages, salary or social welfare, etc) and deduct from it certain allowances.

Capital resources, other than the home, are also taken into account when assessing financial eligibility. If the value of those resources exceeds €320,000, then that party will not qualify for legal services from the Board. Capital resources include property other than the family home, cars, cash, investments, and any other resource that has a value. Allowances are given for certain debts, such as credit union or bank loans that may be offset against capital for the purposes of calculating disposable capital.

Criminal legal aid

If a defendant in criminal matters does not have the means to pay for legal representation, then the State is obliged under Art.38 of the Constitution to provide that legal representation. See *State (Healy) v Donoghue* [1976] I.R. 325.

As already noted, legal aid in criminal matters was introduced by the Criminal Justice (Legal Aid) Act 1962 and extended by the Criminal (Procedure) Amendment Act 1973. However, despite the introduction of those legislative provisions, the existence of a general right to criminal legal aid was not acknowledged until the decision of the Supreme Court in *State (Healy) v Donoghue* (as cited above), where it was stated that there is a need to put the defendant on equal terms with the prosecution. Without legal representation, an ordinary person without any experience of criminal law and court proceedings would be at a serious disadvantage. However, the Supreme Court decided that it is only in certain circumstances that somone has a constitutional right to legal representation. There is no *absolute* constitutional right to it.

Criminal prosecutions first come before the District Court, and it is at this stage that a party is entitled to apply for legal aid. If a charge carries a possible prison sentence and the defendant is not legally represented, the District Court judge is required to inform that defendant that he/she may be entitled to legal aid. If a defendant wishes to be legally represented and claims that he/she cannot afford it, the judge must consider whether that defendant qualifies for free legal aid. In making a decision the judge must consider the following:

- Whether the defendant's means are sufficient to enable him/her to pay for legal aid.
- Whether it is in the interest of justice that the defendant should have legal aid in the preparation and conduct of their defence.

The judge will also assess the seriousness of the case. Here the judge will consider the real possibility of the accused receiving a prison sentence or large fine if convicted. If the offence is not a serious one, the judge may grant legal aid in exceptional circumstances. Such exceptional circumstances may, inter alia, include that the accused is very ill, is immature, lacks any or sufficient formal education, suffers from emotional difficulties, lacks the mental capacity to understand the nature of the charge against him or her and the ability to deal with the trial.

In summary, if the offence is a serious one and the accused cannot afford to pay for their own legal representation, then the court should grant a legal aid certificate.

In some cases, however, where a Legal Aid Certificate is not available, a person may be entitled to apply for free legal representation under another scheme such as the Attorney General's Scheme.

There is no appellate procedure against the refusal of criminal legal aid. However, a further application may be made in the higher court when the matter is sent forward for trial.

Legal aid granted in the District Court only covers District Court proceedings. If a defendant is sent forward to a higher court by the District Court it will be necessary to apply to that higher court for legal aid for their trial. It is very unlikely that the higher court would refuse to grant a legal aid certificate if the District Court has already granted a certificate.

Free Legal Aid Centres

Free Legal Aid Centres (FLAC) were established in 1969. Founded by law students, FLAC is an independent human rights organisation dedicated to the realisation of equal access to justice for all. To this end it offers some basic, free legal services to the public.

The Centres' main attributes are that:

- They concentrate their work on four main areas: legal aid, social welfare, credit and debt and public interest law;
- They have become increasingly involved in credit and debt issues. They support money advisors and members of the public and aim to provide useful information on rights and entitlements through research and publications;
- They seek to help keep the public informed of their legal rights and provide technical legal support in the area of credit and debt law to advisors from MABS and the Citizens Information Board. They also produce publications on issues such as moneylending and the law;
- They are working in the area of public interest law for the benefit of vulnerable and disadvantaged people; and
- They are staffed on a voluntary basis by law students and practising lawyers.

In addition, FLAC operate a fund collecting system collecting donations from, for example, practising lawyers.

Precedent

8

The Doctrine of Precedent

The first thing students should note about precedent is that the common law as a source of law is sometimes referred to as precedent.

The doctrine of precedent means that the decisions of earlier cases, if sufficiently like the case in hand, should be repeated in the case at hand.

In a legal system where lower courts are required to follow decisions of higher courts, that system is said to have a doctrine of precedent. The maxim of stare decisis, meaning let the decision stand, is the underlying principle of the doctrine of precedent. The doctrine of precedent, in essence, is that it is necessary to abide by former precedents when the same points arise again in litigation. As regards courts of coordinate jurisdiction, there is an expectation rather than a requirement that decisions of earlier cases will be followed.

The benefit of a doctrine of precedent is that it brings clarity and certainty to the law. At least, that is the theory.

Although precedent is a feature of both a common law legal system and a civil law legal system, because the common law is effectively judge-made law as opposed to law enacted by a legislature, precedent has much more significance in a common law system.

When courts follow their previous decisions within more or less well-defined limits they are said to be operating a doctrine of precedent. The doctrine of precedent is that cases must be decided the same way when the material facts are the same; this does not mean where *all* the material facts are the same, but rather where all the legally material facts are the same.

In the Irish legal system the District Court is bound by decisions of the Circuit Court, the Circuit Court is bound by decisions of the High Court, and the High Court is bound by decisions of the Supreme Court. This rule, which is the first and foremost rule of the doctrine of precedent, is well settled, is rarely questioned by the courts, and is usually adhered to.

In *McDonnell v Byrne Engineering Co Ltd*, *The Times*, October 3, 1978, the Supreme Court criticised the High Court for failing to follow its decision in *Carroll v Clare County Council* [1975] I.R. 230; the court said that this court "will insist that its directions be respected and obeyed".

The case *DPP v O'Sullivan* [2007] IEHC 248, unreported, High Court, July 31, 2007 gives a clear example of the high regard and respect for precedent that the Irish courts have. Here, the High Court indicated its reluctance to follow the decision of the Supreme Court in *DPP (Riordan) v Molloy* [2003] IESC 17, but nonetheless followed it, saying "the decision of the Supreme Court in *Director of Public Prosecutions v Molloy* is binding on this court ...".

TERMINOLOGY

The following are the terminologies of precedent:

- Ratio decidendi;
- Obiter dictum;
- Per curiam;
- Per incuriam;
- *Sub silentio*;
- Res judicata;
- Reverse;
- Overrule;
- Distinguish;
- Semble;
- Quaere;
- Applied; and
- Followed.

Ratio decidendi

Defining the ratio decidendi

Simply put, the ratio decidendi means "the reason for the decision". It is the ratio decidendi of a case that is the binding part of the judgment. It is suggested by academic writers that the term ratio decidendi has two meanings:

(1) The rule of law propounded by the judge as the basis of his ultimate decision of the case.

(2) The rule of law for which the case is of binding authority.

The ratio decidendi may also be described as the material facts plus the decision thereon.

The term ratio decidendi may be used to describe the process of reasoning by which the decision was reached (the descriptive ratio decidendi).

The ratio decidendi is that part of the case that is said to possess authority (the binding authority). It is the rule of law upon which the decision is founded.

In *State (Burke) v Lennon and the Attorney General* [1940] I.R. 136, the release by habeas corpus of an internee detained under Pt VI of the Offences Against the State Act 1939 was ordered, primarily because in the opinion

Gavan Duffy J., "[p]art VI of the Act was repugnant to the Constitution". The decision of the Court was to release the detainee but the reason for the decision was because, "[p]art VI of the Act was repugnant to the Constitution". (Note: this case is used for example purposes only, as the case was subsequently appealed by the respondent to the Supreme Court).

In the case of *Napier v Napier* [1915] L.R. 184, a decree of nullity on the grounds of a wilful and persistent refusal to consummate the marriage was refused on the ground that the civil courts *had no power to alter the law as it was applied prior to 1857* in the Ecclesiastical Courts of the Church of England. The decision was the refusal of a decree of nullity; the reason for the decision was that the civil courts *had no power to alter the law* as it was applied prior to 1857 in the Ecclesiastical Courts of the Church of England.

Discovering the ratio decidendi

When a case is recorded or reported it does not expressly state what is the ratio decidendi. The ratio decidendi has to be discovered by the later courts considering the earlier case, and thus these later courts play a significant role. Discovering the ratio decidendi of a case is not a mechanical process but is a skill that is gradually acquired through practice and study. However, a general description of the technique employed to identify the ratio decidendi can be given.

In order to discover the ratio decidendi of a case you must first separate the law from the facts to which that law is applied. In brief, it can be identified from a study of the material facts of the case and the decision thereon.

EXAMPLE

- Facts A, B and C exist.
- The court finds that facts B and C are material and fact A immaterial.
- The court reaches a conclusion X (e.g. judgment for the plaintiff or the defendant).
- The doctrine of precedent enables us to say that in any future case in which facts B and C are the only material facts that exist the conclusion of the court should be X.
- In any future case where facts A and B and C and D exist, and fact D is held to be material, the first case will not be a direct authority, though it may be of value by analogy.

As to what facts are legally material depends on the particular case.

EXAMPLE

- Case in court—an action where injuries are sustained by the plaintiff through the defendant's negligent driving of a vehicle. The fact that the plaintiff had red hair and freckles, that his name was Smith and that the accident happened on a Friday are or may be immaterial for the rule of law upon which the decision proceeds and may apply equally to a person who does not possess these characteristics and to accidents that happen on other days. However, if the plaintiff was deaf or had impaired vision these characteristics could amount to material facts.
- On the other hand, the fact that the defendant drove negligently and the fact that, in consequence, he injured the plaintiff, are material, and a decision in the plaintiff's favour on such facts will be an authority for the proposition that a person is liable for causing damage through the negligent driving of a vehicle.

Sometimes a later case will pronounce on what that court feels is the ratio decidendi of an earlier case. See for example, *Maurice Colgan v Independent Radio and Television Commission, Ireland and the Attorney General* [1999] 1 I.L.R.M. 22 where O'Sullivan J., considering the decision in *Murphy v Independent Radio and Television Commission* [1998] 2 I.L.R.M. 360, said this "appears to me to be the *Ratio* of the Supreme Court judgment in *Murphy*".

Special considerations apply with regard to multi-judge or collegiate courts such as the Supreme Court, which sits with three or five judges, or a Divisional Court of the High Court, which sits with two judges. Although the Special Criminal Court sits with three judges, only one judgment is delivered, so the special considerations do not apply here.

In a court of three to five judges it is possible for a decision to be arrived at by a majority of say 3–2, with each judge expressing his/her views or reasons in quite different ways.

The ratio decidendi becomes more evident in situations where only one judgment is delivered to which the other judges concur. Where a majority of the judges agree on the reason for the decision, similarly there is no difficulty.

However, where there are multiple judgments, such as when each judge in a three- or five-judge court delivers a separate judgment, it can present problems in identifying the ratio decidendi of the case. In these circumstances you must extract the reason for the decision of each, then select the reason that is either unanimous, or failing unanimity, the reason with the majority support. This unanimous reason or the majority reason forms the basis of the ratio decidendi of the case in hand.

Where there is neither unanimity or majority support for any reason, discovering the ratio decidendi may be achieved by using one of two approaches.

Approach 1: The ratio decidendi *is the sum of all the reasons*. Thus, for example, in a five-judge court, if each of the five judges had a different reason being V, W, X, Y and Z, the ratio decidendi of the case would be VWXYZ, or if three judges had reason X and the other two had V and W, the ratio decidendi would be XVW and so forth. The effect of using this approach is that the case may only be capable of being a binding authority for cases that are identical.

Approach 2: Instead of a ratio decidendi, the case contains a number of rationes decidendi, and the ratio decidendi which has the majority support is selected. This is the approach suggested by Professor Cross (Cross and Harris, *Precedent in English Law*, 4th edn (Oxford: Oxford University Press, 1991)) and the approach which he feels is probably close to what happens in practice. However, this approach will not work in a situation where there are five separate judgments, all with incompatible reasons, because a later court is left with having to select any one of the five different rationes decidendi. In practice, it is in very rare circumstances that five separate judgments will be advanced with different and incompatible reasons.

Dissenting judgments

Dissenting judgments may also be relevant. A dissenting judgment is the judgment delivered by the minority. Whereas these dissenting judgments do not form a binding part of the decision, they are nevertheless highly influential in later cases. For example, the dissenting judgment of Lord Denning in *Candler v Crane Christmas & Co* [1951] 2 K.B. 164 was largely adopted in *Hedley Byrne & Co Ltd v Heller & Partners Ltd* [1964] A.C. 465.

Dissenting judgments can be relevant for several reasons:

1. Dissenting judgments may be relevant in discovering or ascertaining the ratio decidendi of a case.
2. A dissent might be based on a different interpretation of the evidence or on a different evaluation of the legal issues which the case presents, but nevertheless support the propositions of law advanced by the majority. See, for example, the dissenting judgment of Walsh J. in *People (DPP) v Walsh* [1980] I.R. 294.

3. The majority judges might agree on the result, but for conflicting reasons, and the dissenting judgments may assist in identifying the ratio decindendi.

Obiter dictum

Obiter dictum (plural obiter dicta) is a mere saying, a chance remark or a remark in passing which is not essential to the decision in the case. An example of obiter dictum would be a rule of law stated merely by way of analogy or illustration, or a suggested rule upon which the decision is not finally rested.

Obiter dicta, because they are not of direct relevance to the decision, are not binding. However, they may be adopted at the option of the later court. How persuasive they may be on a later court will depend sometimes on the reputation of the judge who delivered the dictum, the eminence of the court and the circumstances in which it came to be pronounced. See *State (Raftis) v Leonard* [1960] I.R. 381, where the judge felt he was not free to adopt his own interpretation in view of obiter dicta in two Supreme Court decisions.

For examples of obiter dicta, see *Ryannair Ltd v An Bord Pleanála* [2004] 2 I.R. 334, where the court refused the relief sought by the applicant because the court held that applicant did not have locus standi, nor had the applicant shown substantial interest (the ratio decidendi), and went on to say obiter that the "applicant did not simply have locus standi by virtue of being a user of the airport ...". In *AA v Minister for Justice* [2005] 4 I.R. 564 refusing the relief sought the court went on to say obiter that the "applicants were entitled to have access to those documents which had the potential to influence the first respondent's decision". These remarks were obiter rather than part of the decision in the case because there was no evidence before the court that such access was denied.

Per curiam

Per Curiam means "by the court" or, as it is more usually understood, in accordance with law. A decision reached per curiam is one made by a judge in accordance with law and where there is more than one judge, assented to by all.

In *Thomas Grimes v Punchestown Developments Co Ltd* and *MCD Promotions Ltd* [2002] 1 I.L.R.M. 409, where the applicant applied for an injunction to stop the respondent from holding a concert on lands at Punchestown it was held per curiam in refusing the relief sought that the "court's general discretion under s.27(1) of the 1976 Act [s.27(1) of the Planning Act 1976, as amended by the local Government (Planning and Development Act) 1994] is not confined to situations in which five years have elapsed". Because it was a correct statement of the law it is said to be per curiam.

In *Re Whitesheet Inn Ltd* [2003] 2 I.L.R.M. 177, it was held per curiam that in "order to be a householder one must be the tenant or holder of premises which are in part a dwelling house and in which a member of the household dwells".

Per incuriam

Per incuriam means otherwise than in accordance with law. A decision of a court is made per incuriam if it fails to apply a relevant statutory provision or ignores a binding precedent. In *DPP v Dillon* (unreported, Court of Criminal Appeal, December 17, 2003), it was held per incuriam that there was a fixed minimum sentence of twenty years for the offence of manslaughter, and because there is no statutory provision that there is a fixed minimum sentence of twenty years for manslaughter, this holding was per incurium.

Sub silentio

Sub silentio, which is Latin for "under silence", can apply in two situations:

- The first is where a court decides a point without its being specifically argued or mentioned in court and is said to have been decided *sub silentio*. A later court is not required to follow it. In *G v An Bord Uchtála* [1980] I.R. 32, Walsh J. spoke both of the right to life of the unborn and the constitutionality of certain decisions made by the Adoption Board even though counsel had not specifically addressed this in their arguments.
- The second situation is where the effect of some decisions may overrule *sub silentio* previous decisions. See for example, *Convery v Dublin County Council* [1996] 3 I.R. 153, where the court held that the decision in *Weir v Dun Laoghaire Corporation* [1983] I.R. 242 was clearly irreconcilable with the decision in *Sunderland v McGreavey* [1987] I.R. 372; [1990] I.L.R.M. 658 and must be regarded as having been reversed *sub silentio* by *Sunderland*.

Res judicata

Res judicata is Latin for "the matter has been decided". Once a decision becomes final and is no longer subject to the possibility of being appealed, the principle of res judicata applies and the parties to the case are bound by the decision and may not, in general, seek to have it re-opened.

Res judicata is the short-hand term for the doctrine of estoppel *per rem judicatam*. The reason for this doctrine is contained in the following two Latin maxims:

1. *Interest rei publicae ut sit finis litium*. It is in the public interest that there should be an end to litigation; and

2. *Nemo debet bis vexaru ori eaden causa*. No party should be sued twice in respect of the same cause or no person ought to be troubled or harassed twice.

See *Dublin Corporation v Building and Allied Trade Union* [1996] 1 I.R. 468; [1996] 2 I.L.R.M. 547.

Reverse

When an appeal is successful, the appellate court is said to have reversed the decision of the inferior court. The initial decision will, thus, cease to have any effect.

Overrule

When an appellate court in a later case considers the earlier decision of a lower court to be erroneous, it may overrule that decision. Its effect, however, is prospective (going forward) only and it does not affect the position of the parties to the earlier case. Simply put, by overruling a case, a court states that it is not to be followed in the future.

Distinguish

Courts prefer to distinguish rather than overrule earlier decisions. A decision is said to be distinguished when a later court decides that, for one reason or another, it is not relevant to the case before it. A case might be distinguished because the later court discovers a material factual difference between the two cases, because different legal issues are involved, or because the statement of law in the previous case is too narrow to be properly applied to the new set of facts. In essence, the subject matter of the two cases is perceived to differ and they are placed in separate conceptual categories.

Quaere

Quaere means to enquire, question or see. It is used to signify doubt or to suggest investigation. See *Sinnott v Quinnsworth Ltd* [1984] I.L.R.M. 523, where quaere, per McCarthy J., whether the decision in *Reddy v Bates* [1983] I.R. 141 laid down a principle regarding the awarding of compensation.

Semble

Semble means resembles or seems, to imitate or make like. For an example of semble see *State (McDonagh) v Frawley* [1978] I.R. 131.

Stare Decisis

Introduction

Courts of coordinate jurisdiction (courts at the same level) are not bound by their own decisions. However, under the principle of stare decisis, there is an expectation that these decisions be followed. There are necessarily some limits to this principle and courts will depart from it, for example, in cases where the earlier decision of the court was decided erroneously or otherwise in accordance with law or for some other compelling reason.

When considering stare decisis in the Irish courts, a distinction must be made between decisions of the courts prior to 1961 and to pre-1922 decisions of the House of Lords. The reason for this is that in 1961 new courts as envisaged by the 1937 Constitution were established, and although they are identical to the earlier courts, nonetheless they are new courts, and any decisions of the courts prior to 1961 and pre-1922 are not decisions of the new courts established in 1961.

The question of whether pre-1961decisions should be followed first arose in *State (Quinn) v Ryan* [1965] I.R. 110, and later that year in *Attorney General v Ryan's Care Hire Ltd* [1965] I.R. 642, where it was held that a pre-1961 decision could not bind the new Supreme Court. However, in *Mogul of Ireland v Tipperary (North Riding) County Council* [1976] I.R. 260, it was stated that the pre-1961 decisions should only be overruled if they were clearly shown to be erroneous.

Regarding pre-1922 decisions, there are authorities that say they are binding and those that state they are not. For two opposing views, see *Boylan v Dublin Corporation* [1949] I.R. 60 and *Minister for Finance and Attorney General v O'Brien* [1949] I.R. 91.

Whether pre-1922 and pre-1961 decisions are binding or not would appear to be of less significance given the present approach of the Supreme Court to the principle of stare decisis, which is that decisions will be departed from only for compelling reasons.

The Supreme Court and *Stare Decisis*

Initially the Supreme Court adopted the English position on stare decisis which was a strict approach and which essentially meant that the expectation that decisions of earlier courts be followed was to be satisfied. In the case of *State (Quinn) v Ryan* [1965] I.R. 110, a more relaxed approach to stare decisis was adopted by the Supreme Court. The reasons given for the change in attitude was explained thus: stare decisis cannot be anything more than judicial policy, albeit strong judicial policy, and, being a common law principle, may be unsuitable in constitutional cases.

Following the decision in *State (Quinn) v Ryan* [1965] I.R. 110, it may be said authoritatively that the Supreme Court is not bound by its own decisions. However, the court made it clear in this case that the "advantages of *stare decisis* are many and obvious so long as it is remembered that it is a policy and not a binding unalterable rule" and that the court would only depart from an earlier decision for "the most compelling reasons". As already noted, compelling reasons would be where a decision was decidedly erroneously, per incuriam or where a decision is anachronistic (unsuitable for modern times).

An example of the Supreme Court departing from an earlier decision may be seen in *McNamara v Electricity Supply Board* [1975] I.R. 1, where the court refused to follow *Donovan v Landy's Ltd* [1963] I.R. 441 on the basis that the latter was wrongly decided.

It appears that a five-judge Supreme Court will more easily depart from a decision of a three-judge Supreme Court. See *Hamilton v Hamilton* [1982] I.R. 466, where the court said a decision of a Supreme Court sitting with three judges was law "unless and until a different conclusion is reached by a full court". See also *Doyle v Hearne* [1987] I.R. 601, which reinforces this position.

The High Court and *Stare Decisis*

Whether the High Court is bound by its own decisions is not clear-cut. First, is it a High Court sitting with one judge or a High Court sitting as a divisional court with two judges? Secondly, is it hearing a case at first instance or on appeal? Thirdly, is it hearing a civil or criminal matter? The desirability of following decisions of courts of coordinate jurisdiction was emphasised by the High Court in *Walsh v President of the Circuit Court and the DPP* [1989] I.L.R.M. 325. In *Irish Trust Bank Ltd v Central Bank of Ireland* [1976–1977] I.L.R.M. 50, it was stated that unless an earlier decision could be clearly shown to have been wrongly decided, a court of coordinate jurisdiction should follow it.

In *People (Attorney General) v Moore* [1964] Ir. Jur. Rep. 6, it was held that when High Court is sitting as the Court of Criminal Appeal it is free to depart from its earlier decisions. Nonetheless, it is clear that it will only do so in appropriate cases and where there is cause, reason or necessity to so do.

The position of stare decisis when the High Court is hearing an appeal from the Circuit Court has not been judicially determined. However, it may be said that a decision of the High Court on the hearing of an appeal from the Circuit Court is binding on the Circuit Court, as there is no reason why these appellate decisions should not enjoy the same status as decisions of High Court at first instance.

Clearly, higher courts are not bound by the decisions of the District Court and Circuit Court, these courts being inferior courts. Nonetheless, the decisions of these courts are a persuasive authority and judges in the higher courts do not like to disturb a decision of a lower court and will not do so without reason. The higher court may follow the decision of the lower court. Where there are conflicting decisions it may select one, it may ignore a decision altogether or it may decide to overrule it.

None of these actions will be taken lightly and will be done only where there is some compelling reason. See *Finlay v Murtagh* [1979] I.R. 249, where the decision in *Somers v Erskine* [1943] I.R. 348 was overruled, the compelling reason being that it had been wrongly decided and was not compatible "with modern developments in the law of torts".

Where there are conflicting authorities on a topic it is a good opportunity to have the matter sorted out or cleared up by a higher court.

Foreign courts

Whereas an Irish court is not bound by a decision of foreign court, nonetheless decisions of other common law jurisdictions can be highly persuasive on an Irish court, particularly where there is no precedent on a particular issue in the Irish jurisdiction. That it is not to say that they should be followed.

As to whether English decisions should be followed has received much judicial attention in Ireland. There are divergent views on the issue. In *Irish Shell Ltd v Elm Motors Ltd* [1984] I.R. 511, the notion that decisions of English courts should only be rejected where there were compelling reasons for so rejecting was criticised. This court stated that although English decisions have often proved to be of great service they, nonetheless, were not binding upon Irish courts. In a series of cases such as *Boylan v Dublin Corporation* [1949] I.R. 60, *Thomso Sparebank v Beirne (No.2)* [1989] I.L.R.M. 257, and *M McC v J McC* [1994] I.R. 293 it was stated that decisions of English courts are at least persuasive on Irish courts.

Law Reports

Recording of court decisions is important in a legal system which is required to operate a doctrine of precedent, and is necessary for the lower courts to be aware of the decisions of the higher courts. Decisions of the higher courts are recorded and the most important cases decided by those courts may also be reported.

Recorded decisions
Recorded decisions may be found on the Courts Service website (*http://www.courtsservice.ie*) and in the Law Library on a legal data base called JILL (judgments in the law library).

Reported decisions
Not all cases are reported; cases reported will be those of legal interest. In Ireland cases are reported in the following series:

- The Irish Reports (I.R.);
- The Irish Law Reports Monthly (I.L.R.M.); and
- Irish Law Times Reports.

There are also the various Digests.

The Irish Times newspaper publishes reports of cases weekly on a Monday which are referred to as the Irish Times Law Reports. These may be cited in court as they are reported by practising barristers.

Decisions of other common law jurisdictions which can be persuasive on Irish courts, particularly English decisions, are reported in a series called the All English Reports (All E.R.).

Without this accurate reporting of judicial decisions the system of precedent would be almost inoperable.

Case-law may also be accessed on legal databases such as LEXIS-NEXIS, Justis, the British and Irish Legal website (BAILI) and the Irish Government website, *http://www.irlgovii.ie*.

A report typically will set out the title of the case, state which court the case was tried in, a headnote setting out the legal issues, a synopsis of the facts, the legal submissions or arguments of counsel for both sides and the decision of the court.

The *Irish Reports* are published by The Incorporated Council of Law Reporting Ireland.

The *Irish Law Reports Monthly* are published by Thomson Reuters Round Hall.

Various other specialist areas of law have journals which report cases, for example the *Employment Law Reports* and the *Irish Employment Law Journal*, published by Thomson Reuters Round Hall.

The Personnel of the Law

The personnel of the law are the judges, barristers, solicitors, County Registrars, District Court Clerks, court clerks, the Attorney General, the Director of Public Prosecutions and An Garda Síochána. The jury also plays an important role.

The Judiciary

The judiciary are one of the three organs of State, the other two being the Legislature (the Oireachtas) and the Executive. It is the judges who administer justice in the Irish legal system. Judges apply the law and interpret it when necessary.

Appointment of judges

Article 34.1 of the Constitution provides, inter alia, that justice shall be administered by judges appointed in the manner provided by the Constitution. Judges of all courts shall be appointed by the President on the advice of the Government (Art.35.1 of the Constitution).

Under the Courts and Court Officers Act 1995 (the "1995 Act") (Pt IV of the Act) a Judicial Appointments Advisory Board was established. Those persons eligible and wishing to become judges must now apply to this Board. The Board will submit the names of those persons it considers suitable for appointment to judicial office to the Minister for Justice, Equality and Law Reform (s.16 of the 1995 Act). The Minister will then advise the President on the person to be appointed.

Qualifications

Persons eligible to become judges are barristers, solicitors and County Registrars. There are certain requirements in terms of professional practice.

Judges of the District Court

A person who is a practising barrister or solicitor for not less than ten years is qualified for appointment as a District Court judge, or, if not a practising barrister or solicitor at the material time, has had ten years' practising experience and holds an office to which only practising solicitors or practising barristers would be appointed to (s.29(2) and (3) of the Courts (Supplemental Provisions) Act 1961).

Judges of the Circuit Court

Section 5 of the Courts and Court Officers Act 2002, which amends s.17 of the 1961 Act, provides that the following persons are eligible for appointment as a judge of the Circuit Court:

- A person who is for the time being a practising barrister or practising solicitor of not less than ten years' standing.
- A judge of the District Court.
- A County Registrar who practised as a barrister or a solicitor for not less than ten years before he/she was appointed County Registrar.

Judges of the Superior Courts

According to s.4 of the Courts and Court Officers Act 2002, which amends s.5 of the 1961 Act, the following persons are qualified for appointment as judges of the Supreme Court and the High Court:

- A person who is for the time being a practising barrister or practising solicitor of not less than 12 years' standing but who has practised as a barrister or a solicitor for a continuous period of not less than two years immediately before such appointment shall be qualified for appointment as a judge of the Supreme Court or the High Court.
- A person who is or was at any time during the period of two years immediately before the appointment a judge of the European Court of Human Rights, the International Criminal Court, the European Court of Justice, the Court of First Instance or an Advocate-General and who was a practising barrister or practising solicitor before appointment to the office.
- A person who is or was at any time during the period of two years immediately before the appointment a judge of an international tribunal in accordance with the International War Crimes Tribunals Act 1998 and who was a practising barrister or practising solicitor before appointment to the office.
- A person who is a judge of the Circuit Court for not less than two years.

Retirement, resignation and removal of judges

Retirement

- A judge of the District Court must retire at 65 years of age;
- A Circuit Court judge must retire at 70 years of age; and
- Judges of the High Court and Supreme Court must retire at 70 years of age.

Resignation

Resignation or vacation from office is also provided for. Thus a judicial office held by any person may be vacated by resignation in writing addressed to the President and transmitted to the Taoiseach (s.6 of the Courts (Establishment and Constitution) Act 1961).

Removal

Article 35.2.5.4° provides that a judge of the Supreme Court or High Court shall not be removed from office except for stated misbehaviour or incapacity and then only on resolutions passed by the Oireachtas. While the Constitution does not provide that Circuit Court judges may be removed for stated misbehaviour or incapacity, they may be so removed by virtue of legislation (s.39 of the Courts of Justice Act 1924).

In the case of District Judges, there are statutory mechanisms less drastic than removal. Where the Chief Justice is of the opinion that the conduct of a District Judge is such as would bring the administration of justice into disrepute, the Chief Justice may interview the judge privately and inform him of such opinion, but no further sanction is provided for (s.21 of the Courts of Justice (District Court) Act 1946).

The independence of the judiciary

A popular question on a legal systems examination paper is to discuss the independence of judges or the independence of the judicial function. Students make a common mistake here by writing solely on the doctrine of the separation of powers. That is not what this question is about. It is about those provisions that provide for and seek to ensure judicial independence.

The independence of the judiciary, which is an important concept, is dealt with principally in Art.35.2.5° of the Constitution, although it is also referred to in Arts 35.3, 35.4 and 35.5.

That judges should be independent in the exercise of their judicial functions, subject only to the Constitution and the law, is provided for in Art.35.2 of the Constitution. Article 69 and part of Art.68 of the 1922

Constitution also provided for judicial independence. In a dissenting judgment in *O'Byrne v Minister for Finance* [1959] I.R. 1, Lavery J. said that it is clear from the 1922 Constitution "that the judicial power of the State should be vested in judges set apart in many important ways from the life of the community and denied important civil rights in order that they should be independent in the exercise of their function".

In order to achieve this judicial independence, Art.35.3–35.5 provides for such matters as security of tenure of judges, non-reduction of judges' salaries and judicial ineligibility of judges for election to the Oireachtas.

Article 35.3 provides that no judge shall be eligible to be a member of either House of the Oireachtas or to hold any other office or position of emolument. Thus, judges cannot become a member of the Dáil or Seanad and remain in office as a judge, and they cannot take on any other paid appointment as this would have the potential to impinge on their judicial independence. See *In re the Solicitors Act and Sir James O'Connor* [1930] I.R. 623.

Article 35.4.1° provides that a judge of the Supreme Court and the High Court shall not be removed from office except for stated misbehaviour or incapacity, and then only on resolutions passed by the Oireachtas. Although Art.35.4 refers specifically only to judges of the Supreme Court and the High Court, the same procedure would undoubtedly have to be followed for District Court and Circuit Court judges as these judges are declared to "hold office for the same tenure as the judges, of the Supreme Court and the High Court" by the Courts of Justice Act 1942 and the Courts of Justice (District Court) Act 1946 (see *Magee v Culligan* [1992] 1 I.R. 223).

Article 35.5 provides that the remuneration of a judge shall not be reduced during his continuance in office. See *O'Byrne v Minister for Finance* [1959] I.R. 1.

In addition, the provisions listed below tend to ensure judicial independence:

- The common law rule that acts done or words spoken by a judge in his judicial capacity are absolutely privileged (see *Tughan v Craig* [1918] 1 I.R. 245; and *Byrne v Ireland* [1972] I.R. 241).
- The traditional rule to the effect that there should be no order for costs against members of the judiciary in judicial review applications where they had acted bona fide. See *McIlwraith v Fawsitt* [1990] 1 I.R. 343, where the Supreme Court re-affirmed this rule.
- Judges have a right to protect their independence by summary punishment for contempt. See *State (Director of Public Prosecutions) v Walsh* [1981] I.R. 412, where it was held this right was implicit in Art.35.2. See also, *Re Kelly v Deighnan* [1984] I.L.R.M. 424, where the Supreme Court said that

the High Court enjoyed a jurisdiction to deal summarily with cases of contempt "to protect the administration of justice".

The Master of the High Court

The role of Master of the High Court was created by the Court Officers Act 1926 (s.3). The Act sets out the powers, authority, duties and functions of the Master (s.5). The court in which the Master sits is known as the Master's Court. The Master has jurisdiction in uncontested cases, and may take accounts, conduct inquiries and make interlocutory orders such as orders compelling discovery and orders compelling replies to particulars. He/she may enter judgment in summary debt proceedings. He/she has jurisdiction to appoint a medical examiner in nullity proceedings. He/she is empowered to exercise limited functions and powers of a judicial nature within the scope of Art.37 of the Constitution (s.24 of the Courts and Court Officers Act 1995).

The Master is appointed by the Executive Council and holds office at their pleasure and must retire from office on attaining the age of seventy years.

The Barrister

The role of a barrister

A barrister (or counsel) represents his/her client as an advocate in court. A barrister provides independent legal advice and legal opinions regarding a proposed action in court or on almost any legal issue. The barrister drafts the pleadings, prepares legal submissions and questions witnesses in court by way of examination-in-chief and cross-examination. A well-argued case can be influential in persuading a judge that your case is a good one. A barrister's training in advocacy and, above all, experience, can make a big difference to the outcome of a case.

Armed with specialist skills in court practice and in negotiation, a barrister is in a position to advise his or her client on the strengths and weaknesses of their case and advise whether to fight the case or settle it through negotiations.

Increasingly, barristers are retained to represent their client's case outside the conventional courtroom setting such as in mediations, arbitrations, tribunals, disciplinary hearings and a broad spectrum of public and private inquiries.

When representing the prosecution it is the duty of the barrister to present the case for the prosecution with a view to trying to secure a conviction. However, his/her primary duty is to assist in the administration of justice. He/she must operate within the limits of the rules of evidence and within the limits of the trial procedures. In the presentation of the prosecution case, he/she must endeavour to be fair and impartial in the presentation of the facts of the case.

When representing the defence, the barrister enjoys much greater freedom than the prosecution barrister. His/her duty is to secure an acquittal for his/her client. Similar to the prosecution barrister, he/she must operate within the rules of evidence and within the rules of trial procedures.

How to qualify as a barrister

There are three stages to qualifying as a barrister. These are:

1. The academic stage;
2. the vocational stage; and
3. the apprenticeship stage.

The academic stage

During this stage, would-be barristers must either have an approved law degree or the Diploma in Legal Studies from the King's Inns. Details of the accredited or approved law degrees will be found on the King's Inns website, *http://www.kingsinns.ie*.

The vocational stage

This stage involves the would-be barrister undertaking the one-year full-time course of Degree of Barrister-at-Law at King's Inns. Admission to this degree course is after completion of the academic stage, having passed the entrance examination which is held annually.

Those who pass the Degree of Barrister-at-Law will be "called to the Bar of Ireland" by the Chief Justice of Ireland and are eligible to become a member of the Law Library which is a prerequisite to becoming a practising barrister.

Once a barrister becomes a member of the Law Library they are free to take up work in their own right, and to start building up a practice. In Ireland, practising barristers are sole traders.

The apprenticeship stage

The first year of the barrister's practice must be spent as a pupil (also known as a one-year "pupillage") with an approved Dublin-based practitioner. During the year of pupillage (known as "devilling") the pupil or devil must carry out their master's instructions and learn about the nature of professional practice.

THE SOLICITOR

THE ROLE OF THE SOLICITOR

Solicitors have a very wide range of functions. Solicitors meet the clients at first instance. A solicitor may give legal advice about non-contentious matters, such as buying a house or flat or drafting a will. A solicitor may act as an agent or representative in commercial transactions. A solicitor may also give legal advice and represent parties in relation to a dispute or disagreement with another party. A solicitor may give legal advice about taking or defending a case.

It is the solicitor who manages and controls the case and represents either the plaintiff or defendant. For example, the solicitor for the plaintiff will send communications on behalf of the plaintiff to either the defendant or the solicitor for the defendant or vice versa. The solicitor will file all of the necessary court documents. The solicitor will organise the witnesses and the necessary proofs as directed by the barrister.

If it is necessary to involve a barrister in the case, the solicitor will instruct and "brief" the barrister by sending him/her all of the necessary documents and information.

A solicitor may represent a client in court, although in the Circuit Court, the High Court and the Supreme Court, a barrister will usually be engaged and it is becoming increasingly more regular to find the barrister in the District Court.

Unlike barristers, solicitors are allowed to join together to form partnerships or companies and they are allowed to advertise their services. The Law Society sets down rules and regulations about how solicitors may conduct their business.

HOW TO QUALIFY

A person wishing to become a solicitor must complete an apprenticeship of at least two years and must pass the examinations set by the Law Society at Blackhall Place in Dublin. The various stages are:

1. The preliminary examination
2. The final examination—first part (FE–1)
3. The training programme
4. The professional practice course 1 (PPC 1)

The preliminary examination

This is an examination for non-graduates held once a year, usually in March. Candidates must be at least 21 years old. The examination consists of the following: papers in English, Irish Government and politics and general knowledge.

The following are exempt from the preliminary examination: university graduates from Ireland and the United Kingdom or holders of degrees (regardless of the discipline) awarded by the Higher Education and Training Awards Council (HETAC). Holders of degrees from other universities may apply to the education committee for exemption from the preliminary examination. Law clerks and legal executives can apply to the education committee for exemption from the preliminary examination if they have at least five years' experience and hold a diploma in legal studies, or an equivalent qualification, or have in excess of ten years' experience (diploma in legal studies not required).

Holders of other qualifications can apply to the education committee for exemption on the basis of such qualifications.

The final examination—first part (FE–1)

This is the entrance examination to the Law Society of Ireland. Only those who have passed or gained exemption from the preliminary examination can sit this examination.

The training programme

The in-office training period is the core of the training programme. All trainees are required to have general practice experience, to include experience in conveyancing, landlord and tenant law, litigation, wills, probate and administration of estates.

The professional practice course I (PPC I)

Eligible applicants for the PPC I must have:

- Passed, or gained exemption from, the preliminary examination;
- Passed the final examination—first part;
- Found a suitable (practising) solicitor to act as a training solicitor.

The PPC I takes place annually.

THE JURY

The common law countries believed that the best way of dealing with matters of fact in a trial was to bring into the court twelve citizens selected at random so that they can bring their accumulated experience of life, wisdom and common sense to the case—in other words, a jury. Article 34.5 of the Constitution now gives any person charged with a criminal offence, other than a minor offence, a right to trial by jury. The purpose of a jury trial is to ensure a fair trial in accordance with law (see *O'Callaghan v Attorney General* [1993] 2 I.R. 17).

The function of the jury is to determine the guilt or innocence of an accused person on the facts of the case, the judge being the trier of the law. Thus the jury must take the law from the judge whether they agree with it or not.

It is not necessary that a jury be unanimous in its verdict. In a civil trial, a verdict may be reached by a majority of nine of the twelve members. In a criminal case, a verdict need not be unanimous. Where there are not fewer than eleven jurors, ten of them may agree on a verdict after considering the case for a reasonable time being not less than two hours.

The jury has no role in sentencing. Their role is:

- To decide which of the facts of the case are proven.
- To take directions relating to law from the trial judge.
- To remain impartial and independent.
- To remain uninfluenced by any person.
- To keep statements made in the jury room confidential.

The selection process for juries is carried out in accordance with the provisions of the Juries Act 1976 (the "1976 Act"). This Act repealed the Juries Act 1927, which provided that only landowners of land of a certain rateable valuation could serve on juries and it also had a provision exempting women from jury service. The Act of 1927 was repealed following a challenge under the equality guarantee in the Constitution (see *De Búrca v Attorney General* [1976] I.R. 38).

Qualification for jury service is set out in the 1976 Act. A juror must be an Irish citizen and must be 18 years of age but not more than 70 years of age. Persons must be entered on the Dáil Register of Electors. A person who meets those requirements may be liable for jury service unless disqualified. Persons who are disqualified from serving on a jury are persons who have been convicted in Ireland (sentenced to life imprisonment or for a term of 5 years or more), persons who have committed capital offences, or persons who, in the past ten years, have served a sentence or any part of a sentence for a term of at least three months.

The President and all persons concerned with the administration of justice are ineligible, such as judges, coroners, solicitors, barristers, Gardaí and court personnel. Certain other people may also be ineligible, such as a person suffering from a disability or incapacity (for example, being unable to read, deafness or mental health).

A person can seek to be excused from jury service. Section 9 of the Act recognises that there could be considerable disruption to public services if certain people are called for jury service, for example doctors, nurses, dentists, teachers, lecturers, students, or members of either House of the Oireachtas. Persons who have served on juries in the past three years are entitled to seek to be excused if a jury summons is served on them. A person who serves on a jury which goes on for a long period may, at the discretion of the trial judge, be excused from further service for life.

The jury must be representative of the community, otherwise it will fall foul of Art.38 of the Constitution. Previously, jurors were selected in consecutive order from the juror books, but the court took the view that this method of selection failed to produce representative juries. On a representative jury see *MacCartaigh v Eire* (unreported, Supreme Court, July 15, 1998); and see *R v Ford* [1989] Q.B. 868.

Today the selection process is organised by the County Registrars. Local authorities give copies of the current electoral registers to each County Registrar from which is drawn up the jury panel. This procedure has to be a random selection and a non-discriminatory selection. In drawing up a panel the County Registrar will exclude any person that the County Registrar knows to be disqualified. A sufficient number to provide juries for all cases to be tried for a given term will be chosen. More than 12 names are put on the panel because there will be applications to be excused and further candidates will be excused by the trial judge on the day of the trial. When the panel has been determined by the County Registrar, he/she will cause a summons with a cover letter to be sent out to each person on the panel. The letter explains the effects of ss.7, 8, 9, 35 and 36. Sections 7, 8 and 9 cover ineligibility, disqualification and excuses. Sections 35 and 36 outline penalties.

The summons requires the person to whom it is addressed to attend at a particular courthouse on a particular day for jury service. When the people are assembled in court before selection takes place it is customary for the judge to address the panel of jurors before that process gets underway. The judge will usually give a brief statement about the nature of the case that is to be tried. The judge will then invite any potential juror who has concerns about his/her qualification for jury service to communicate that fact to the judge if their name should be called out in the selection process. It is an important feature of the jury that they should be disinterested and impartial. If they know anybody involved in the case they should let the court know so that they can be omitted.

The actual selection of the jury will then start with the Registrar calling out juror's names. Names are selected randomly from a box. The name will be called out and that person steps forward and comes to the top of the courtroom. At that point there may be challenges. Any challenge must be made before the juror is sworn in.

There are two types of challenge:

(1) Peremptory challenge;
(2) Challenge for cause.

Peremptory challenge: Under the Act, both prosecution and defence can challenge up to a maximum of seven jurors without having to show cause. This is known as the right to peremptory challenge. Because no reasons are given, the challenge cannot be subjected to any argument or any questioning. Any juror who is challenged is then excluded from the jury. These challenges are based on subjective standards such as appearance, age, sex, address or employment.

Challenge for cause: Both prosecution and defence enjoy the right to challenge any number of jurors for cause shown. If the challenge is successful, the person is excluded from serving on the jury.

The Parties to a Case

In civil matters, the parties to a case are called the plaintiff and the defendant or the applicant and the respondent. There is a further party called a petitioner.

In criminal matters, the parties to a case are called the prosecutor and the accused or defendant.

Plaintiff

A plaintiff is the person bringing the procedings and applying for relief or remedy against another person in a civil action.

Defendant

A defendant is the alleged wrong-doer; a person against whom civil proceedings are instituted or against whom a prosecution is brought.

Applicant

Similar to plaintiff.

Respondent

Similar to defendant.

Petitioner

The party who brings the petition. Somewhat similar to a plaintiff.

Prosecutor

The party bringing a criminal action against a defendant. Usually the Director of Public Prosecutions (DPP) but other persons are authorised in law to prosecute certain criminal actions.

There may be other parties, such as a third party or a notice party.

Third party

A third party is a person or party against whom a defendant may have a claim arising out of the same of set of circumstances. A plaintiff may adopt the third party as a further defendant. Alternatively, the defendant may seek a contribution or indemnity from the third party.

Notice party

A notice party is a person or party whom, although not a party to an action, may be directly affected by the outcome. For example, the outcome of an action brought by a second spouse against his/her spouse as to validity of his/her divorce from the former spouse may have implications for the former spouse. A court may direct the joining of a person or party as a notice party.

Next friend

A next friend is an adult who takes responsibility for the conduct of legal proceedings on behalf of a minor (infant) or some other party who is not capable in law of being responsible for the action, such as a person of unsound mind. A parent will usually be the next friend of their infant children.

McKenzie friend

A McKenzie friend (or McKenzie man) is a person who sits beside a lay litigant. The role of the McKenzie friend is to assist the lay litigant by quietly prompting or giving advice and keeping notes of the proceedings. The name comes from the 1971 case of *McKenzie v McKenzie* [1971] 3 All E.R. 1034.

County Registrars, District Court Clerks and Court Clerks

County Registrars

County Registrars are appointed directly by the Government. The County Registrar has responsibility for the administration and management of Circuit Court offices. They also perform a number of quasi-judicial functions which are conferred on them by statute, for example, entering judgments in default and the taxation of costs. They are independent in the exercise of quasi-judicial functions. Appeals against their decisions are made directly to the Circuit Court judge.

Some County Registrars deal with probate matters. Most County Registrars perform duties in relation to land registry. Other functions of the role are to act as returning officers during general elections.

District Court clerk

The District Court clerk is appointed pursuant to Court Officers Act 1962. He or she:

- administers the work of the District Court;
- can be called out to arrange special sittings of the District Court at night or over the weekends;
- signs all summonses on behalf of the DPP and, where summons are issued from the Central Administration Processing Unit, they must bear the name of the appropriate clerk;
- is a registrar of Clubs and Licensed Premises and must keep a Register of all such licences in his/her area as he/she may be called upon to give evidence of these in court; and
- in family law maintenance matters has authority to prosecute in his/her own name a defaulting maintenance debtor.

Court clerks

The functions and work of court clerks are many and varied. The court clerk is the Registrar of the court sittings. As such, they take charge of the preparation and order of business in the court list, including calling the cases, swearing in the witnesses, recording the orders of the judge, and preparing warrants and bonds for signature.

The court clerk liaises with the judge, Gardaí, prison officers, solicitors, probation officers and all concerned parties in relation to the cases. This is the most public face of the court clerk. Other duties are those concerned with the administration of the court business—the office work, the issuing of notification of court results and fines, issuing warrants for non-payment, receipting money, endorsing driving licences, certifying parties for legal aid and preparing draft court orders.

All in all, the court clerk is an important member of the courts' structure with many responsibilities.

The law officers of the state

The law officers for the state are the Attorney General and the Director of Public Prosecutions. There is also an officer known as the Chief State Solicitor.

The Attorney General

The Attorney General is a creature of the Constitution (see Art.30 of the Constitution). The Attorney General is the legal adviser to the Government and is therefore the chief law officer of the State. The Attorney General is appointed by the Taoiseach and leaves the office if the Government changes. Usually the person appointed is a barrister or solicitor. While the Attorney General is not a member of the Government, he/she traditionally attends at Cabinet meetings.

If a person or body is suing the State, the Attorney General is added as a defendant and is the person upon whom proceedings are served.

The role of Attorney General includes:

- Advising the Government on all the constitutional and legal issues which arise in connection with Government. This includes advising as to whether proposed legislation complies with the Constitution or with Ireland's obligations under European Union law or under other international treaties to which Ireland has acceded.
- Representating the public in all legal proceedings for the enforcement of law in Ireland and the assertion or protection of public rights.
- Acting as lawyer for the State in virtually all civil litigation in which the State or its officers are official parties.
- Giving legal advice on matters that are submitted by government departments and offices and drafting necessary legal documents.

The Director of Public Prosecutions

The Office of the Director of Public Prosecutions was created in 1974 by s.2 of the Prosecution of Offences Act 1974. The DPP is thus a creature of statute. Prior to the creation of that office, prosecutions were taken in the name of the Attorney General.

When the Office of the DPP was created, prosecutorial functions were transferred from the Attorney General to the DPP. However, for some offences the DPP requires the consent of the Attorney General in order to prosecute.

Whilst nearly all prosecutions are taken in the name of the DPP, two Acts confer the prosecutorial function on the Attorney General for certain offences that may give rise to sensitive political issues. (See the Fisheries Amendment Act 1978 and Extradition Acts 1965–2000).

It is DPP who decides whether to prosecute or not in criminal matters. As a general rule the decision of the DPP on this issue is not subject to judicial review.

Certain statutes provide that certain persons and certain specified bodies can prosecute offences. Those usually empowered by statute are Ministers of various government departments and local authorities. Notwithstanding this authority under the Act, if any of the authorised bodies do not bring a prosecution, it is open to the DPP to prosecute.

The Chief State Solicitor

The functions of the Chief State Solicitor and his/her office include:

- The provision of a solicitor service in all civil courts in which any government department or other State authority is involved.
- Conveyancing of State property and related property law services.
- The furnishing of legal advice on various subjects and the drafting of the necessary accompanying legal documents.
- The preparation and presentation of all prosecutions initiated by ministers or government departments.
- Acting as agent of the Government before the European Court of Justice.
- Acting for the State in enquiries under the tribunals of enquiry and supplying legal staff to act for the tribunals.
- Advising and preparing commercial contracts for government clients.
- Advising and representing the State parties in asylum and refugee law cases.
- Acting for the State in extraditions, European arrest warrant proceedings, mutual assistance cases, and also cases involving the transfer of sentenced prisoners.

Generally, the solicitor service for the prosecution of crime is provided by the DPP through the Chief Prosecution Solicitors Office. In the case of prosecutions arising outside of Dublin, the solicitor service continues to be provided by the local state solicitor service.

An Garda Síochána

An Garda Síochána, which was formed in 1922, is the national police force. It has responsibility for carrying out all policing duties in the State. In addition, it provides state security services and carries out all criminal and traffic law enforcement. "An Garda Síochána" means "guardians of the peace".

The first piece of Irish legislation relating to the Gardaí and describing their functions is the Garda Síochána (Temporary Provisions) Act 1923.

Structure of An Garda Síochána

The Minister for Justice, Equality and Law Reform is accountable to the Oireachtas for the performance of An Garda Síochána. A Garda Commissioner is, however, appointed by the Government and is responsible for the day-to-day running of the force. The Commissioner has Deputy Commissioners and Assistant Commissioners.

For policing purposes, Ireland is divided into six regions, each of which has a Regional Assistant Commissioner. Each region is made up of a number of Garda Divisions. A Chief Superintendent is in charge of a Division, which is in turn made up of Districts.

Each District has a Superintendent, in charge. Districts are divided into sub-districts, each normally the responsibility of a Sergeant. Each sub-district usually has only one Garda station. The number of Gardaí in a sub-district can vary.

Below Assistant Commissioner, the Garda rank structure is as follows:

- Chief Superintendent
- Superintendent
- Inspector
- Sergeant
- Garda

The basic command unit is the District. The Superintendent in charge is also known as the District officer and has a number of specific functions relating to such matters as licensing of bars and the issuing of firearms certificates.

Garda power to search and arrest

The Gardaí have powers to arrest if they suspect the commission of a criminal offence. They also have powers to search person and property. In some cases, the Gardaí can arrest and carry out searches without a warrant.

Gardaí have powers to issue summons in the name of the DPP and to charge persons with alleged offences.

The Probation Service

The probation service plays an active role in the criminal court. It is part of the Department of Justice, Equality and Law Reform but is located separately and is managed on a day-to-day basis by the Director of the probation service.

Its role is to assess and manage offenders in the community on behalf of the courts service and the prison service, and in the process help to make society safer. The Probation Service also work in prisons and detention centres.

The functions of the probation service are:

- The effective assessment and management of offenders.
- Facilitating the integration of ex-offenders.
- The provision of probation supervision, community service, offending behaviour programmes and specialist support services to both adult and young offenders, which aim to stop the commission of further offences.

Many of the activities of the probation service are carried out in liaison with other agencies, in particular with the the Department of Justice, Equality and Law Reform, the irish youth justice service, the courts service, the irish prison service, an Garda Síochána and a range of other organisations in the statutory sector, as well as in the voluntary and community sector.

The probation service delivers services to individuals, communities, courts and prisons across the entire country. While the services are organised nationally, they are managed and delivered locally.

Additionally, the probation service co-operates with criminal justice agencies in other jurisdictions, especially in cases where offenders move between countries.

Remedies and Enforcement

Introduction

Remedies, also referred to as relief or redress, are the outcome in civil law actions, whereas enforcement and sentence/punishment are the outcomes in criminal law actions.

Civil law remedies may be the remedies of the common law courts, the courts of equity/chancery (equitable remedies) or a combination of both. The common law remedy is damages, whereas the equitable remedies are injunctions, specific performance and rescission. Declaratory relief (declarations) may also be available in appropriate cases. Equitable remedies are discretionary, which means that even though a litigant may be successful, the court retains a discretion as to whether that litigant should be granted the remedy or not. However, the discretion must be exercised fairly and justly.

The outcome of a criminal law action will be a sentence which may be a fine, imprisonment, a probation order, a community service order, a compensation order or a combination of these orders.

A further remedy may be available in applications for judicial review where orders of certiorari, mandamus, prohibition or declaration may be granted. In appropriate cases damages may be awarded in a judicial review application.

Civil Law Remedies

In civil law actions, as already noted, if the plaintiff wins his/her case, the remedy, relief or award will be one, or a combination, of the following:

- Damages
- Injunction
- Specific Performance
- Recission
- Declaration.

Damages

Damages is monetary compensation awarded by a court to a successful plaintiff. Damages are intended to put the successful plaintiff in the position he/she would have been in if the tort or wrong complained of had not been committed. In the case of breach of contract, damages is intended to put the successful plaintiff in the position he/she would have been in if the contract had been performed.

The underlying principle is that the sum awarded should place the injured person in the position he or she was in before the wrong was committed, in so far as money can so do. This is known as the principle of restituto in integrum. See *Wall v Hegarty* [1980] I.L.R.M. 124.

In cases involving financial loss, an award of damages is relatively straightforward. However, the principle of restituto in integrum cannot be applied in full in all cases and is particularly difficult in cases of non-financial loss such as personal injuries, where it is often impossible to repair injuries fully or at all. In such cases the award of damages reflects an attempt to compensate for the loss suffered.

As a general rule a successful plaintiff is entitled to full compensation for his/her losses. However, a plaintiff is expected to mitigate his/her losses. This means taking all steps reasonable and possible to reduce the loss. For example, if a plaintiff is suing for wrongful dismissal, that plaintiff is expected to seek alternative employment and thus reduce the financial loss resulting from being unemployed.

The amount of damages awarded may also be reduced due to any contributory negligence by the plaintiff. For example, if a plaintiff failed to wear a seat belt in an accident, an amount of in or about ten per cent may be deducted from the final award in respect of the plaintiff's contributory negligence by failing to wear a seat belt.

In Ireland, damages are awarded on the basis of a once-off lump sum award, rather than "staged" or annual payments.

The law of tort recognises three categories of damages that may be awarded to a successful plaintiff:

- General damages;
- Special damages; and
- Aggravated/exemplary damages.

General damages

General damages are awarded in respect of losses that the law presumes are the natural and probable consequence of a wrong. General damages also refers to a monetary sum awarded for injury, pain and suffering, loss of amenity and reduction in life expectancy. The Injuries Board (see p.144) book of quantum sets out amounts in respect of general damages under three categories for the various types of bodily injury. These three categories are (i) substantially recovered, (ii) significant ongoing, and (iii) serious/permanent condition. The courts are not bound by the amounts set out in the book of quantum.

The book of quantum can be accessed on the Injuries Board website *http://www.injuriesboard.ie*.

Special damages

Special damages are damages special to the particular case. Special damages may include such items as loss of earnings (past and future), medication, physiotherapy and other such treatments, doctors' fees, damage to clothing, vehicles or other belongings.

Aggravated or exemplary damages

Aggravated or exemplary damages are damages that are awarded when the conduct of the defendant or the circumstances whereby the injury was caused to the plaintiff increase the injury by subjecting the plaintiff to humiliation, distress or embarrassment, particularly in such torts as assault, false imprisonment and defamation.

Case-law on damages

The courts have played a major role in the development of the law of damages. It is important, therefore, that the student is familiar with the important cases on the topic. These are:

- *Wall v Hegarty* [1980] I.L.R.M. 124 (see above);
- *Reddy v Bates* [1984] I.L.R.M. 197;
- *Cooke v Walsh* [1984] I.L.R.M. 208;
- *Sinnott v Quinnsworth Ltd* [1984] I.L.R.M. 523;
- *Kennedy v Ireland* [1987] I.R. 587;
- *McEneaney v Monaghan County Council* [2001] IEHC 114; and
- *Nolan v Murphy* [2005] IESC 17.

In *Reddy v Bates* [1984] I.L.R.M. 197, the Supreme Court reduced damages awarded by the High Court, stating that where the damages have been assessed under several headings, the total sum and the income it could generate should be considered to ascertain whether such sum is out of all proportion to the circumstances of the case. Matters to be taken into consideration in calculating an award of damages are the risk of unemployment, redundancy, illness, accident or marital prospects. Damages should be sufficient to cover all losses and bodily needs and to enable the plaintiff to live in comparative comfort having regard to the disability. In reviewing damages, the awards for past and future losses should be considered both separately and as a whole.

In *Cooke v Walsh* [1984] I.L.R.M. 208, the Supreme Court said that in ascertaining damages for future loss of earnings, a judge must take into account the risk of unemployment or redundancy that economic forecasts indicated as likely for the present and foreseeable future. Whether the plaintiff would have been required to pay income tax and other deductions from his wages also was to be taken into account.

In *Sinnott v Quinnsworth Ltd* [1984] I.L.R.M. 523, the Supreme Court said that in assessing damages, regard should be had to ordinary living standards in the country, general income levels, and how the plaintiff might reasonably be expected to spend money. On the facts of a particular case, other matters might arise for consideration in assessing what level of damages would be considered as reasonable. However, a yardstick of reasonableness must be applied if reality is to be retained.

In *Kennedy v Ireland* [1987] I.R. 587, it was held that in certain exceptional circumstances, *punitive* or *exemplary damages* may also be awarded.

In *McEneaney v Monaghan County Council* [2001] IEHC 114, the High Court stated that it was unreasonable for the defendants to bear the costs of a special road traffic accident rate in hospital over and above the ordinary rate, and the rate to be charged for the cost of a hospital stay was an economic rate for that hospital and that the charge could not be arbitrary, unjust or partial.

Nolan v Murphy [2005] IESC 17. This is the first Irish Supreme Court case on the appropriate level of damages to be awarded in civil proceedings for sexual abuse. The court decided that the principles applicable to the awarding of damages for physical injury (as set out in *Sinnott v Quinnsworth* [1984] I.L.R.M. 523) were equally applicable to damages for sexual abuse. Thus the amount of damages had to be fair and reasonable to cover pain and suffering in the past and into the future and must have regard to ordinary living standards, general income level and ways in which the plaintiff might spend the money.

Shortt v Commissioner for An Garda Síochána, Ireland and the Attorney General [2007] IESC 9. The Supreme Court decision in this case has implications for litigation against the State where damages may be awarded.

This judgment is the most important one on aggravated and exemplary damages in recent times.

INJUNCTIONS

The remedy of injunction was developed by the courts of equity to prevent one party from acting in such a way as to interfere with the rights of another. An injunction is an order of the court that directs a person to do, or to refrain from doing, a specified act. For example, it can be used to prevent acts of trespass.

Injunctions need to be considered from a temporal aspect and from the aspect of the various types of injunction available.

Temporal aspect

Injunctions from a temporal aspect are:

1. *Interim injunction*

An interim injunction lasts from the time it is granted by the court up to the hearing of the interlocutory injunction. An interim injunction is usually granted ex parte.

2. *Interlocutory injunction*

An interlocutory injunction lasts until the trial or further order. Before a court will grant an interlocutory injunction, the applicant must satisfy the test set out in the case of *Campus Oil v Minister for Industry and Energy* [1983] I.R. 88 which is as follows: there must be a serious and fair question to be tried; the balance of convenience must lie in favour of granting the injunction; damages must not be considered an adequate remedy; and the applicant must give an undertaking as to damages.

3. *Perpetual injunction*

A perpetual injunction, as the name suggests, lasts forever. It will usually be one of the orders sought at the time of the trial of the action.

Types of Injunctions

The various types of injunction are:

- Prohibitory injunction (restraining or forbidding);
- Mandatory injunction (directing something be done);
- *Quia Timet* injunction (used in respect of a threatened wrong);
- *Mareva* injunction (used to freeze assets); and
- *Anton Piller* injunction (used to seize articles or documents).

Prohibitory injunction
A prohibitory injunction prohibits. It seeks to restrain the defendant from doing something or from persisting, continuing or repeating the wrongful act.

Mandatory injunction
A mandatory injunction mandates. It seeks to direct or order the defendant to do something or to end a wrongful state of affairs.

Quia timet injunction
Quia timet is Latin for "because he fears". A *Quia timet* injunction is sought in order to restrain an anticipated wrong. It is granted by the court where the applicant can show that there is imminent danger of a substantial type or that the injury, if it is allowed occur, will be irreparable.

Mareva injunction
The *Mareva* injunction is an injunction that enables the court to freeze the assets of a defendant (whether resident within the jurisdiction of the court or not) in order to prevent the defendant from removing his assets abroad to avoid the enforcement of an award of damages made to a plaintiff. See *Mareva Compania Naviera SA v International Bulkcarriers SA* [1975] 2 Lloyd's Rep. 509. This remedy has in recent times become very popular in the commercial world.

Anton Piller injunction
An *Anton Piller* injunction is an injunction which enables a plaintiff or his/her representatives to enter the defendant's premises to inspect or take away material evidence that the defendant might wish to remove or destroy in order to frustrate the plaintiff's claim. This injunction is commonly used in cases where the copyright of video films or tapes is alleged to have been infringed. See *Piller (Anton) KG v Manufacturing Processes Ltd* [1976] Ch. 55 (C.A.).

SPECIFIC PERFORMANCE

A decree of specific performance is an order to a party to a contract to fulfil his/her obligations under the contract. In other words, it is an order to perform the contract. A condition precedent to obtaining a decree of specific performance is that there exists a contract which should be enforced.

A decree of specific performance is commonly sought in relation to contracts for the sale of land or building of properties. For example, a court may order a reluctant seller to complete the sale of a property. The order of specific performance is not considered suitable in all types of contract. For example, it is not usually available in relation to employment contracts, because here the parties would essentially be forced to perform a contract for personal services. Neither is it generally available in cases where damages is an adequate remedy.

Rescission

Rescission is a remedy used in the law of contract. It means the setting aside of a voidable contract. This remedy has the effect of unwinding (rescinding) the contract and treating it as if it had never existed. There are limits to a litigant's right to an order of rescission. Rescission will not be granted where restitution in integrum is not possible. In other words rescission will only be granted where it is possible to restore the parties to the same position they were in at the time of entering into the contract.

Declaration

A declaration, or declaratory relief, is a private law or public law remedy. A declaration is essentially an answer to a question regarding the legality of a state of affairs or to the rights of the parties. The question to be answered must be real and not theoretical. It can be a stand alone remedy, and this has been made clear by Ord.19 r.29 of the Rules of the Superior Courts 1986, which provides that no objection may be taken solely on the basis that a declaration is the only remedy sought.

A declaration is a flexible remedy because it can be tailored to the particular circumstances of a case.

Irish courts now have a liberal approach to the grant of declarations, although this was not always the case. See *Transport Salaried Staffs' Association v Córas Iompair Éireann* [1965] I.R. 180, where the court said that "the virtues of the declaratory action are more fully recognised than they formerly were ...".

Declaratory relief may be sought in an application for judicial review. (On judicial review, see below). Examples of declarations that might be sought are declarations invalidating Acts of the Oireachtas; declarations invalidating delegated legislation; declarations invalidating criminal convictions; declarations invalidating administrative action for want of jurisdiction or fair procedures; and declarations determining the scope of a party's entitlement or rights.

Judicial Review

Judicial review is first and foremost a remedy. Although it may sometimes have the same effect as an appeal it is not an appeal, but an application to the court for a remedy. Judicial review dates back to Anglo-Norman times when it was known as the prerogative writs. After 1922 it became known as state side orders and in 1986, under the Rules of the Superior Courts, became known as judicial review.

The application for judicial review is made to the High Court which has exclusive jurisdiction in judicial review applications. Order 84 of the Rules of the Superior Courts 1986 governs the procedure for judicial review. It is a two-stage process; the applicant must at the first stage obtain the leave of the High Court to bring the actual application, and the second stage is the hearing of the application itself.

There are four types of orders or remedies available to the applicant in judicial review proceedings. There is a further remedy available under Ord.84 known as habeus corpus. The four orders are:

1. *Certiorari*
2. *Mandamus*
3. *Prohitition*
4. *Quo Warranto.*

A declaration is also available in a judicial application. In appropriate cases damages may be awarded in a judicial review action.

Remedies or orders available in a judicial review application are discretionary.

CERTIORARI

An order of certiorari is an order which quashes a decision of a lower court or tribunal where that court or tribunal, for example, has been found to have acted ultra vires (outside its powers). See, for example, *State (Cussen) v Brennan* [1981] I.R. 181, where the Supreme Court granted an order quashing the decision of a body appointing a candidate other than the applicant as a paediatrician because the Minister for Health had prescribed that the successful candidate should have a knowledge of Irish in circumstances where he did not have the power to so prescribe.

MANDAMUS

This is an order directed to a court or tribunal ordering it to fulfil a lawful obligation that it is not carrying out or that it is carrying out in an incorrect manner. See, for example, *State (Keller) v Galway County Council* [1958] I.R. 142, where the court granted an order directing a medical officer in Galway County Council to rehear an application for disability allowance on the basis that when the application was first heard and refused the medical officer had taken into account irrelevant matters.

PROHIBITION

An order of prohibition is directed at a court or tribunal preventing it from exercising its powers, either completely or until certain conditions have been met. See *State (Williams) v Kelleher* [1983] I.R. 112, where an order was made forbidding (prohibiting) the continuance of a preliminary examination under the Criminal Procedure Act 1967 in respect of an indictable offence because the applicant had not been served with a complete book of evidence as required by the Act. (Note: the preliminary examination has since been abolished).

QUO WARRANTO

Quo Warranto is the means whereby an applicant might challenge the validity of the respondent's appointment to an office or the respondent's qualifications for that office. Despite the recommendation of the Law Reform Commission that *Quo Warranto* be abolished, it still remains. However, it is not widely used today.

HABEUS CORPUS

Habeus corpus is used to challenge the validity of the detention of a person generally held in official custody. Habeus corpus derives from the royal prerogative writ and was then obtained by petitioning the sovereign. Today it is done by way of application to the High Court under Ord.84 of the Rules of the Superior Courts 1986. On application, the High Court orders the custodian to appear and justify the detention.

CRIMINAL LAW PENALTIES AND ENFORCEMENT

Criminal law enforcement is by way of sentence, which is essentially a penalty. The trial judge decides what penalty to impose but may be fettered to a degree by statute regarding the minimum or maximum penalty a judge may impose. In some cases there is a mandatory penalty leaving no discretion whatsoever to the judge.

Where the defendant is convicted the judge may impose one, or a combination, of the following:

- A fine;
- Imprisonment;
- A probation order;

- A community service order;
- A compensation order.

Fines

The fine imposed cannot exceed the maximum amount provided for in statute. Before imposing a fine, the court has to have regard to the means of the accused. The court will have regard to the manner in which the case was met by the accused. If the accused pleads guilty he/she will usually get credit for this by way of the imposition of a lower fine. Any order imposing a fine must provide for time to pay and also make provision for what is to happen in the event of default in payment, which is generally a number of days in prison.

Imprisonment

If a person is convicted and sentenced on a summary offence, the term of imprisonment can vary from up to six or twelve months, but it cannot exceed twelve months. If the person is before the court on a number of charges and the judge decides on imprisonment in respect of all or some of the charges, the sentences will run either consecutively or concurrently.

A judge may impose a sentence of imprisonment but decide to suspend it. Suspension will be on the basis of certain conditions being met. For example, the convicted person may be required to enter into a bond to be of good behaviour and to keep the peace. If any of the conditions are breached the suspension is lifted and the sentence of imprisonment may be activated.

Detention

A male person who is not less than 17 years of age and not more than 21 years of age upon conviction must be detained rather than imprisoned. Detention may be in St Patrick's Institution in Dublin or it may be in residential homes or detention centres. The detention centre is the option used for offenders under 12 years of age.

There is no detention for female offenders. Female offenders who are 17 years of age or over go to prison and sometimes female offenders between 15 and 17 years of age find themselves in prison because of the lack of alternative suitable places for them.

Probation

A judge may decide to give the defendant the benefit of the Probation of Offenders Act 1907. Under this Act the judge can either dismiss the charge or discharge the accused conditionally. This is usually done where the court is of the opinion that having regard to the character of the accused, the age, health, mental condition, the trivial nature of the offence, or the extenuating circumstances in which the offence was committed, it is appropriate to apply the Act. The court may require the offender to enter a bond to be of good behaviour for a period.

Where a charge is dismissed under this Act, although the charge was proven against the accused, a conviction is not recorded, but if the offender comes before the court again evidence may be given that the Act was applied on a previous occasion. The benefit of the Act may be granted more than once. The absence of a previous conviction does not entitle a defendant to the benefit of the Act. See *Gilroy v Brennan* [1926] I.R. 482.

Although not expressed in the Act, it would appear that an order under the Act is not appropriate where a sentence for the offence in question has been fixed by statute.

Community service order

When a judge decides that although the appropriate penalty is imprisonment or detention, he/she may nonetheless impose a community service order. The jurisdiction for this is found in the Criminal Justice (Community Service) Act 1983. There are a number of requirements that must be met. The accused must be 16 years of age or more; the offence must be one for which the appropriate punishment is imprisonment/detention; the offender must be an appropriate person for a community service order (this is decided on the basis of a report from the probation officer); the accused must consent to the order being made; and the court must be satisfied that a suitable arrangement can be put in place for the person as a community service worker.

If a community service order is made it requires the offender to carry out hours of community service not less than 40 hours and not more than 240 hours.

Compensation order

A compensation order is an order directing the convicted person to pay compensation to the victim for injury, damage or loss to the person or property. The ordering of compensation in criminal matters by the courts has been around for some time but was given statutory footing by the Criminal Damage Act 1991 and by the Criminal Justice Act 1993.

A compensation order may be made in lieu of the imposition of another penalty or in addition to that penalty.

Sometimes the court orders compensation and adjourns the case for sentencing with an implication that if the compensation is duly paid up the sentence will be more lenient than would otherwise be the case.

Alternative Dispute Resolution

11

Introduction

Alternative dispute resolution provides alternative ways of resolving disputes other than going to court. Thus, *alternative* means alternative to the law courts. Today there is a whole range of bodies, organisations and agencies that are engaged in alternative dispute resolution.

The Injuries Board provides an alternative to court proceedings in cases of personal injury action.

Alternative dispute resolution can include referral of a dispute to arbitration, referral to a statutory tribunal, referral to an ombudsman, referral to a commissioner, a trade association, a regulator, or to one of the consumer protection organisations.

Examples:

- A party with a dispute arising from contract may have agreed to put a dispute, present or future, to arbitration.
- A party with an employment dispute may refer the matter to the Rights Commissioner, the Labour Court or the Employment Appeals Tribunal.
- A residential tenant or landlord with a grievance can refer the matter to the Residential Tenancies Board.
- A party claiming discrimination may have a dispute which is referable to the Equality Authority.
- A party who is in dispute with a telecommunications provider may refer the matter to ComReg (the Regulator of telecommunication services).
- An asylum seeker/refugee may refer the matter to the Refugee Appeals Tribunal.
- A party may put a matter in dispute to one of the ombudsmen.
- A party with a financial, insurance or pension grievance may refer the matter to the Financial Services Ombudsman.

- A party refused access to information to which there is an entitlement under the Freedom of Information Act 1997 may refer the matter to the Information Commissioner.

In some of the above examples a party with a grievance or claim has no option but to put the matter before the body in question.

The main benefit of using alternative dispute resolution is that, at least in theory, it is quicker, easier and less expensive than going to court.

Alternative dispute resolution organisations are flexible and are impartial. They must also ensure the effectiveness of their settlement procedure and encourage both sides to co-operate.

There is also what is known as mediation: both parties involved in the dispute agree to use a neutral third party to help solve, or mediate, the dispute. The terms of agreement are decided between the parties with the help of the mediator. Generally, decisions made in mediation are not legally binding but they can be made so if both parties agree to it.

ARBITRATION

Arbitration, as a form of dispute resolution, can have many advantages over litigation or other forms of adjudication and dispute resolution in appropriate cases. Advantages of arbitration are:

- Flexibility: The arbitrator is typically chosen by the parties or nominated by a trusted third party.
- Specialist knowledge: The arbitrator will usually have a specialist knowledge of the field of activity.
- Efficiency: The parties can decide on the location, language and to a great extent, the timing, of the hearing to facilitate the parties and their witnesses.
- Informality: The process is less formal than court.
- Certainty and finality: The arbitral award is final, binding and enforceable and may only be appealed to the courts on limited grounds.
- Speed: Speed can result in cost savings.
- Privacy: Arbitral awards are private and do not become binding precedents.

Sources of arbitration: In Ireland, arbitration was governed by the Arbitration Acts 1954, and 1980, which provided a legal framework for both domestic and international arbitrations. The Arbitration (International Commercial) Act 1998 introduced the United Nations Commission on International Trade Law (UNCITRAL) Model Law as the procedural framework for international arbitrations.

Arbitration is now governed by the Arbitration Act 2010 which came into law on June 8, 2010. The Act governs all arbitrations commenced after that date. It repeals the Arbitration Act 1954, the Arbitration Act 1980 and the Arbitration (International Commercial) Act 1998. The purpose of the Act is to apply the United Nations Commission on International Trade Law (UNCITRAL) Model Law on International Commercial Arbitration to all arbitrations which take place within the State. At present that law applies in relation to international commercial arbitration only. Section 6 of the Arbitration Act 2010 provides that the model law shall have the force of law in the State.

The model law is set out in a series of Chapters.

Chapter I concerns general provisions covering, inter alia, key definitions and rules of interpretation and the extent of court intervention.
Chapter II focuses on the form of the arbitration agreement.
Chapter III deals with the composition of the arbitral tribunal.
Chapter IV deals with the jurisdiction of the arbitral tribunal.
Chapter IVA deals with interim measures and preliminary orders.
Chapter V deals with the conduct of arbitral proceedings.
Chapter VI deals with the making of an award and the termination of proceedings.
Chapter VII specifies the grounds on which an award may be set aside.
Chapter VIII deals with the recognition and enforcement of arbitration awards.

Arbitration is a suitable process for the resolution of most types of dispute. There are, however, some exceptions. These exceptions include disputes with third parties where injunctive relief is required; disputes relating to the validity or accuracy of public registers, such as patent or trademarks registers; criminal matters; and matrimonial and other "family law" disputes.

The decision to refer a dispute to arbitration is made at the contract stage. The jurisdiction of the arbitration tribunal is based on the written contract of the parties. The contract must contain an arbitration clause and the clause must cover the dispute in question.

The arbitration clause, as already noted, must be in writing and may address either present or future disputes. An agreement to refer an existing dispute to arbitration is often referred to as an "ad hoc reference".

Example of an arbitration clause:

> Any dispute or difference, present or future, of any kind whatsoever or howsoever arising or occurring between the parties herein regarding or in relation to any thing or matter arising under, out of, or in, connection with this agreement shall be referred to arbitration.

If the parties agree that the matter is to go to arbitration in the event of a dispute then they must abide by that agreement. Should one of the parties decide to issue legal proceedings in the ordinary courts in respect of a dispute that was agreed would be referred to arbitration, the other party may bring an application to stay the parallel court proceedings. This is known as the primacy of arbitration. See, for example, *Gleeson v Grimes* (unreported, High Court, November 1, 2002).

The arbitrator's decision is final and binding. Thus there is no appeal (s.27 of the Arbitration Act 1954). However, the High Court has power in some very limited circumstances to set aside an award of an arbitrator. The established grounds for setting aside an award are:

- Where the arbitrator has misconducted himself/herself.
- Where there is some patent defect or error on the face of the arbitrator's order.
- Where the arbitrator has made a mistake and wishes to have it corrected.
- Where new evidence has come to light which could not have been discovered prior to the making of the award.
- Where there has been a procedural mishap.

It was held in *McCarrick v The Gaiety (Sligo) Ltd* (unreported, High Court, April 2, 2001) that the right to set aside was not limited to the established grounds. Thus the above is not a closed category.

OMBUDSMEN

Ombudsmen provide another useful method of alternative dispute resolution. Currently in Ireland there is statutory provision for four ombudsmen:

1. The Ombudsman
2. The Financial Services Ombudsman
3. The Legal Services Ombudsman
4. The Garda Ombudsman.

The Ombudsman is an official created by statute and appointed to investigate individuals' complaints about bad administration, especially that of public authorities. In Ireland, the Ombudsman investigates complaints made by members of the public who feel that they have been unfairly treated by certain public bodies.

There is a fifth Ombudsman, the European Ombudsman, who investigates complaints involving any of the EU institutions.

Generally, Ombudsmen will take on a case only if a party remains dissatisfied with an organisation, having exhausted that organisation's internal complaints mechanism.

1. The Ombudsman

The Ombudsman Act 1980 established the Office of Ombudsman. The Act sets out the role and powers of the Ombudsman as regards the examination and investigation of complaints made to the Ombudsman.

The Ombudsman is independent in the performance of the functions of the Ombudsman but is required to report to the Oireachtas.

The Ombudsman may investigate an action where a complaint has been made and, having carried out a preliminary examination of the matter, if it appears to her/him that the issue complained of has adversely affected the complainant and where the action was or may have been taken without proper authority, taken on irrelevant grounds, taken as a result of negligence or carelessness, based on erroneous or incomplete information, taken improperly or discriminatorily, based on an undesirable administrative practice, or otherwise, is contrary to fair or sound administration.

There is a preliminary examination stage, the purpose of which is two-fold; to establish in a quick and informal way whether a formal investigation is warranted and to enable complaints to be resolved with the minimum of formality where appropriate. Investigations are conducted in private and the Ombudsman may decide his/her own procedure for conducting such investigation. The Ombudsman is given powers to require any party with relevant information to furnish that information or to appear in person.

The Ombudsman is empowered to make recommendations only. These recommendations or findings are not binding but they will be persuasive in some cases. When the Ombudsman carries out an investigation the complainant must be informed of the outcome of such investigation and of any response or submissions received regarding the recommendation made by the Ombudsman. If it appears to the Ombudsman that the response to a recommendation is unsatisfactory, the Ombudsman has power to submit a report on the matter to the Oireachtas.

An adverse finding regarding any person or body will not be published in a report without first giving that person or body an opportunity to respond to the matter.

The Ombudsman is required to make an annual report on the performance of the functions of the office of the Ombudsman to the Oireachtas.

The following matters are excluded from examination or investigation by the Ombudsman:

- If the matter is before the courts.
- If the complainant has a statutory right of appeal to the courts.
- If there is a right of appeal to an independent appellate body.
- If the complaint relates to recruitment or terms or conditions of employment.
- If the complaint relates to aliens or naturalisation.
- If the complaint relates to a pardon or to remission of prison sentences or other court penalties.
- If the complaint relates to the administration of prisons.

Since 1985, An Post and the Health Boards (now the Health Services Executive) have been brought within the remit of the Ombudsman. Not all complaints relating to the HSE, however, will be within the remit of the Ombudsman.

Although the Office of the Ombudsman is to be welcomed and although the remit of the Ombudsman has been extended over the years by legislation, there nonetheless remains areas where reform would be welcome, such as the fact that in Ireland the Ombudsman lacks jurisdiction in the area of asylum unlike other EU Member State colleagues.

2. The Financial Services Ombudsman

It was felt in the late 1990s as part of the overall enhanced regulatory framework for the financial services sector, including the establishment of a Financial Regulator, that a statutory Ombudsman scheme for all providers of financial services with statutory powers was necessary. (See the McDowell report of 1999.) This is now the position enshrined in legislation. See s.16 and Schs 6 and 7 of The Central Bank and Financial Services Authority of Ireland Act 2004.

The Financial Services Ombudsman Bureau became operational on April 1, 2005.

The role of the Financial Services Ombudsman, who is a statutory officer, is to deal independently with complaints from consumers about their individual dealings with all financial services providers that remain unresolved by these said providers. The Ombudsman is an impartial arbiter of unresolved disputes. The Ombudsman deals with complaints or disputes by mediation and, where necessary, by investigation and adjudication. An adjudication of the Financial Services Ombudsman may be appealed to the High Court, otherwise it is final and binding.

The service provided to the complainant by the Financial Services Ombudsman is free. The Financial Services Ombudsman is funded by levies from the financial services providers. The existing voluntary ombudsman schemes for credit institutions and insurance schemes were subsumed into it and the number of financial service providers covered by its remit was expanded considerably.

The following financial service providers may be subject to investigation by the Financial Services Ombudsman:

- Banks
- Building societies
- Insurance companies/pension providers
- Credit unions
- Mortgage, insurance and other credit intermediaries
- Stockbrokers
- Pawnbrokers
- Money lenders
- Bureaux de change
- Hire purchase providers
- Health insurance companies
- Retail credit firms
- Home reversion firms

3. THE LEGAL SERVICES OMBUDSMAN

Towards the aim of an enhanced regulatory framework for the legal services sector (essentially services provided by barristers and solicitors) a statutory Ombudsman scheme for providers of legal services with statutory powers was felt necessary.

This scheme is now provided for by the Legal Services Ombudsman Act 2009. Prior to the enactment of this Act, parties with a grievance could refer the matter to the Bar Council of Ireland as regards services provided by barristers and to the Law Society of Ireland where the service provider is a solicitor.

The Act will come into operation on such day or days as the Minister may appoint. (At the time of publishing such day or days has not been appointed).

The Legal Services Ombudsman will be a statutory officer who deals independently with complaints from consumers about their individual dealings with legal services providers.

The following legal service providers may be subject to investigation by the Legal Services Ombudsman:

- The Bar Council of Ireland;
- The Law Society of Ireland;
- Barristers; and
- Solicitors.

According to the Act (s.9(1)) the functions of the Legal Services Ombudsman are:

(a) to receive and investigate complaints,
(b) to review under section 24 the procedures of the Bar Council and the Law Society for dealing with complaints made to those bodies,
(c) to assess the adequacy of the admission policies of the Law Society to the solicitors' profession and of the Bar Council to the barristers' profession,
(d) to promote awareness among members of the public of matters concerning the procedures of the Bar Council and the Law Society for dealing with complaints made to those bodies, and
(e) to carry out any other duties and exercise any other powers assigned to the Ombudsman by this Act.

The Legal Services Ombudsman will keep under review the procedures of the Bar Council and of the Law Society for receiving and investigating complaints in relation to barristers and solicitors respectively.

- The Legal Services Ombudsman will have all powers that are necessary for the performance of the functions of the Office of Legal Services Ombudsman (s.9(2) of the Act).

- The Act provides that Legal Services Ombudsman shall be independent in the performance of the functions of the office (s.10 of the Act).
- The Act envisages liaison between the Ombudsman, the Bar Council of Ireland and the Law Society of Ireland.
- The Legal Services Ombudsman may refer questions of law to the High Court.
- The Legal Services Ombudsman must submit a written report to the Minister on the performance of the functions of the office during that year. Within two years from the date of being appointed, the Legal Services Ombudsman must submit to the Minister a report on the following matters:

    (a) the effectiveness of the office of Legal Services Ombudsman, *and*
    (b) the adequacy of the functions of the office.

The report submitted may contain recommendations for improving the effectiveness of the office of Legal Services Ombudsman.

The Legal Services Ombudsman may additionally make any other reports that he/she considers appropriate for drawing to the Minister's attention matters that have come to the Ombudsman's notice and that, in his/her opinion, should, because of their gravity or other exceptional circumstances, be the subject of a special report to the Minister, and shall make a report on any other matter if so requested by the Minister (s.14 of the Act).

Each year, the Legal Services Ombudsman shall prepare and submit to the Minister a report:

(a) specifying the number of persons admitted to practice as barristers and solicitors respectively during that year, and
(b) containing an assessment as to whether, having regard to the demand for the services of practising barristers and solicitors and the need to ensure an adequate standard of education and training for persons admitted to practice, the number of persons admitted to practice as barristers and solicitors in that year is consistent with the public interest in ensuring the availability of such services at a reasonable cost (s.20 of the Act—*Students should note this provision when considering entry into the profession of barrister or solicitor*).

4. The Garda Síochána Ombudsman

The Garda Síochána Ombudsman Commission is an independent statutory body established under the Garda Síochána Act 2005. It replaced the Garda Síochána Complaints Board since May 9, 2007 but with a much more expanded role. The Garda Síochána Ombudsman Commission provides an independent and effective civilian oversight of policing. It deals with the public's complaints concerning Gardaí fairly and efficiently so that everyone can have confidence in the complaints system.

Under the Act, the Ombudsman Commission is required and empowered to:

- Directly and independently investigate complaints against members of the Garda Síochána;
- Investigate any matter, even where no complaint has been made, where it appears that a Garda may have committed an offence or behaved in a way that would justify disciplinary proceedings;
- Investigate any practice, policy or procedure of the Garda Síochána with a view to reducing the incidence of related complaints.

Three people make up the Garda Síochána Ombudsman Commission.

Complaints must be made within six months of the incident, although the Garda Ombudsman may extend the time limit if there are good reasons. On receiving the complaint, the Garda Ombudsman must decide whether the complaint is admissible and whether it can handle the complaint. To be admissible a complaint must be:

- Made by someone who is entitled to complain;
- About conduct by a Garda that could be considered misbehaviour;
- Made within the acceptable time limit.

If the Garda Ombudsman accepts the complaint as admissible, it may be handled in one of four different ways:

- Informal resolution or mediation;
- Garda investigation;
- Garda investigation under Garda Ombudsman supervision; or
- Investigation by the Garda Ombudsman.

If the complaint is considered less serious it may be resolved through mediation or informal resolution. Both the complainant and the Garda must agree to the complaint being dealt with in this way. A formal investigation may be requested at any stage.

The Garda Ombudsman has developed guidelines for the resolution of complaints through mediation or other informal means. If it is decided to try and resolve a complaint by informal means, this may be undertaken by a Garda Ombudsman Case Officer or by a Garda of supervisory rank. If it is decided to use mediation, the Garda Ombudsman will nominate a trained mediator. The Garda Ombudsman may decide to refer a complaint to the Garda Commissioner.

The Garda Ombudsman may decide to investigate a complaint itself and usually does in the case of serious complaints. It always does so where a complaint involves the death of, or serious harm to, someone due to a Garda operation, or while in Garda custody or care.

If it is found that there was a breach of discipline under Garda disciplinary regulations, the Garda Ombudsman can recommend disciplinary proceedings to the Garda Commissioner. If it is felt that criminal proceedings should be considered, the Garda Ombudsman can send a file on the case to the Director of Public Prosecutions. If there is not enough evidence to support either of these actions, the case may be dismissed. The Garda Ombudsman has no powers to impose penalties or sanctions itself.

The Garda Ombudsman may also investigate the practices, policies and procedures of the Gardaí, if requested to do so by the Minister for Justice, Equalty and Law Reform, and make recommendations in order to reduce or eliminate complaints.

Regulators

Regulators are agencies established by law to oversee specific parts of professions, industry or trade to ensure that they comply with the law. Regulators aim to promote competition while ensuring that vulnerable consumers have sufficient services at reasonable prices. In Ireland, regulators look after areas of public utilities and financial services. For example, ComReg regulates telecommunications in Ireland, the Commission for Energy Regulation regulates the gas and electricity suppliers, the Taxi Regulator regulates the taxi sector and Financial Regulator regulates the financial services sector in Ireland.

The Injuries Board

The Personal Injuries Assessment Board (PIAB), now known as Injuries Board, was established under the Personal Injuries Assessment Board Act 2003 and received state funding to support its establishment. The Board is now self-funding and not reliant on any state funding. The funding of operations is met primarily by levying fees on respondents. Claimants pay an application fee which is currently €50.

Under the Personal Injuries Assessment Board Act 2003, a party intending to seek compensation for a personal injury (other than a personal injury arising out of medical negligence) *must* make an application to the Injuries Board.

The parties to a claim are known as the applicant (plaintiff) and respondent (defendant).

The process of making a claim to the Injuries Board is commenced by the applicant, within two months of the injury complained of, by notifying the respondent in writing of the applicant's intention to make a claim (this is known as the letter of claim). An application is then made to the Board. The application must be made within two years of the injury complained. The following documentation is necessary:

- A completed application form;
- A medical assessment form completed by the claimants treating doctor;
- Payment of €50.

When a claim is submitted it is forwarded to the respondent, who may accept liability, and the Board then assesses the amount of compensation to be paid to the applicant. Claims are assessed on the basis of independent medical report and by reference to the Board's book of quantum. If both parties accept the assessment, the Board issues an Order to Pay.

The Respondent may decline to accept liability, in which case the applicant receives authorisation from the Board to issue court proceedings. No court proceedings in respect of personal injuries to which the Act applies may be issued without this prior authorisation.

In theory, the procedure is meant to reduce the amount of time it takes to finalise a compensation claim and to reduce costs by doing away with the need for lawyers and other experts. Under the court system it can take approximately three years to settle a claim. It generally takes nine months to settle a personal injury claim via Injuries Board.

Most claimants do, however, engage the services of a solicitor.

The Civil Liability and Courts Act 2004 has reduced the limitation period under the Statute of Limitations Act 1957 in respect of personal injuries actions from three years to two years. While the claim is with the Injuries Board the clock for the purposes of the limitation period is stopped.

The Board is staffed by public servants with appropriate legal, insurance and medical expertise to assess compensation. The Board has also established an independent panel of medical experts throughout the country.

Index